TABLE OF CONTENTS

The Science of Psychology EXPOSED
It's All A Fraud!
©2013 Dr. Harry Jay

DISCLAIMER AND TERMS OF USE AGREEMENT:

(Please Read This Before Using This Book)

This information is for educational and informational purposes only. The content is not intended to be a substitute for any professional advice, diagnosis, or treatment.

The author and publisher of this book and the accompanying materials have used their best efforts in preparing this book.

Introduction

"I am not afraid of storms, for I am learning to sail my ship"

As a behavioral scientist, I am constantly being mislabeled as being "part of the problem" rather than being "part of the solution."

I fully understand why, and as you will see after reading this book that there is something terribly wrong with the medical profession and science of Psychology.

I am not a fan of the medical arts including the so-called

mental or mind healing arts.

Even though I am a scientist, I like to think of "scientist" as just a label; I don't fit into any of the labels associated with the medical or mental healing arts.

Candidly, I think I even know why. You see, I am not a medical doctor or psychologist! I am a mental health counselor and behavioral scientist; I practice the procedures of research and scientific analysis by attempting to "disprove" rather than "prove" a scientific theory.

We call this falsification in science.

This is a very important distinction in science and one that most people confuse.

However, as a devout believer in God, I am prejudiced along the lines of what my bible teaches me as it pertains to creation and science. This is where the labels come roaring in…*sigh!*

I have never been very tolerant of the psycho-babble that many social scientists employ to confuse issues – many of which I will bring up in this book.

I am also aware that many of these psycho-babble associates can and do attack me daily because they have no other recourse, yet, none have ever even attempted to refute my premises.

They cannot prove I am wrong so the only thing left to do is discredit and malign.

With all of that said, what I will attempt to do here is provide you with some food for thought and then you can try to prove me wrong too.

My readers are the final court of opinion and always will be for this scientist. I enjoy the feedback I get from my readers.

I think it is important that you understand who you are and why you do the things you do.

I feel that in order to undertake the study of the human mind, basic foundations to this pursuit need to be laid down and organized so that my readers can follow along easily and attentively.

However; with that said, I must also warn that the medical profession vehemently protects its "rice bowl" to a point of being inane.

Remember this: there is no profit in curing anyone only in treatment!

There is no such thing as commercial versus personal psychology.

The mind uses the exact same mechanism to evaluate a personal relationship as it does in evaluating a commercial relationship.

My central premise is simply this: psychology is a fraud! PERIOD!

As I go along, I will outline why I believe this to be the truth.

You can decide for yourself and as always I welcome your comments; just write to me at support@ePubWealth.com

Chapter 1 - We Have Educated Ourselves into Imbecility!

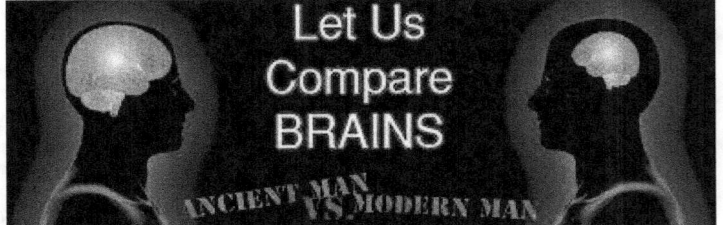

"We have educated ourselves into imbecility," quipped the noted English journalist Malcolm Muggeridge, as he bemoaned the many nefarious ideas that are shaping modern beliefs. Venting an identical disillusionment in his commentary on American culture, George Will averred that there is nothing so vulgar left in our experience for which we cannot transport some professor from somewhere to justify it.

Why this juxtaposing of aberrant behavior with the halls of learning? The answer is well worth pursuing if we are to deal with our present world cultural malaise by understanding its progenitors, and thwart what looms as a future with terrifying possibilities.

It is not unprecedented that as a young nation begins to reach its adolescent years, it craves freedom from any restraint. Emulating a legal proceeding in which an attorney tries valiantly to discredit witnesses who injure his or her case, secular thinkers unleashed a concerted effort to prejudice the minds of this generation. If even a slight doubt could be raised upon any minutiae of theistic belief, it was exultantly implied that the whole worldview should be deemed false. The goal was to forge a new breed of young scholars and opinion-makers who would be perceived as saviors, delivering society from the tyranny of a God-infested past and remaking culture in their own image.

The principal means to accomplish this was to take control of the intellectual strongholds, our universities, and under a steady barrage of "scholarly" attack, to change the plausibility structure for belief in God, so that God was no longer a plausible entity in scholastic settings. This assault on religious belief was carried out in the name of political or academic freedom, while the actual intent was to vanquish philosophically anything that smacked of moral restraint. Unblushingly, the full brunt of the attack has been leveled against Christianity as Eastern religions enjoy a patronizing nod and the protection of mystical license. As for Islam, no university dares offend. Hand-in-hand with this unmasked intellectual cowardice and concealed duplicity came mockery and ridicule of the Christian, which has now become commonplace, a "civilized" form of torture.

In such fashion came the onslaught of all that had gone before; the pen became the sword and the professorial lectern, the pulpit. If young, fertile minds could be programmed into believing that truth as a category does not exist and that skepticism is sophisticated, then it would be only a matter of time before every social

9

institution could be wrested to advantage in the fight against the absolute.

However, over time the sword has cut the hand that wielded it, and learning itself has lost its authority. Today as we look upon our social landscape, the answers to the most basic questions of life, from birth to sexuality to death, remain completely confounded. The very scholars who taught their students to question authority are themselves disparaged by the same measure. No one knows what to believe as true anymore; and if anything is believed, the burden of justification has been removed.

Yet, all is not lost. In spite of the varied and willful attempts made by antitheistic thinkers to undermine the spiritual and to thrust it into the arena of the irrational, or at best deem it a private matter, the hunger for the transcendent remains unabated. After nearly two decades of lecturing on campuses around the world, it is evident to me that the yearning for the spiritual just will not die. In fact, at virtually every engagement I have found the auditorium filled to capacity and the appreciative response quite overwhelming, even in antagonistic settings. There is no clearer demonstration of this unrelenting hunger than the experiences of Russia and China as each has in its own way tried to exterminate the idea of God, only to realize that God rises up to outlive his pallbearers.

Our universities tell a similar story. Though proud skepticism is rife in academic bastions, the human spirit still longs for something more. This tension must be addressed, especially at this time of cultural upheaval, and it is imperative that the answers we espouse meet not only the intimations of the heart but the demands of the mind. The familiar adage rings true: the mind is too great an asset to waste, for it is the command control of each individual life. And it is my desire that each of us may come to recognize the greatest mind of all, even God Himself, whose existence or non-existence is essential to defining everything else.

One major problem in the world today (and this applies especially to "educated" people") is that they are not really very smart. Actually "smart" is not the right word. What I am trying to say is that they are not very perceptive and suffer from a marked inability to look and see things as they actually are.

The reason for this is that they are the most familiar with the ideas and notions of the times, having been thoroughly "educated" (a better word is indoctrinated) into these notions and ideas. This "education" (indoctrination) generally acts to create a set of cultural or "professional" blinders (filters) which prevents the "educated" person from viewing or understanding anything outside of the current "professional" framework that they have been indoctrinated into. It's not that they lack and need more knowledge, but that the knowledge that they do have, in and of itself, acts to prevent them from being able to view and understand anything outside their often limited framework of beliefs and attitudes - a framework that they assume to be all-inclusive and often quite perfect.

The rest of the culture goes along with everything that they promote as "facts" and "truth," because these viewpoints and attitudes tend to be everywhere - newspapers, magazines, TV, schools and colleges. In

fact they are labeled professionals and command respect irregardless of their character.

An Example - Modern Medicine

One example of this is modern western medicine (Allopathy), which is almost completely drug-oriented. Let's begin by understanding the sciences and how they interrelate, and then I will get back to Allopathy and the drug companies.

It is important to understand that all medical sciences and practices come from a religious foundation. From the 5th century BC until the mid-1800s, all medicine was practiced based on humoralistic beliefs and techniques. This practice is attributed to the Greek physician, Hippocrates, but holds a significant resemblance to the ancient Hindu system called the "Ayurvedic" system. Humors are the fluids in the human body. This was the reason a person was "bled," and leeches employed to remove excess fluids. Once this quackery was debunked, western medicine turned to allopathic practice or "Allopathy."

Allopathy is a method of treating disease with remedies that produce effects dissimilar from those caused by the disease itself.

Allopathy is the system of medicine practiced today by medical doctors (M.D.s) and relies solely on scientific experimentation.

Allopathy differs from naturopathy insofar as the former practices curative medicine, and the latter practices preventative medicine. Allopathic medicine uses medications and surgery. Naturopathic physicians employ natural or alternative methods.

12

Homeopathy is a system of medicine, or method of treating disease with remedies that produce effects similar to those caused by the disease itself.

Osteopathy and chiropractic systems are methods using manipulation of the skeleton to cure problematic parts of the body. None of the methods used today regard the "mind" as influencing the healing process. This is very wrong.

*****

Okay, now back to allopathy and the drug companies. The drug companies are the largest supporters of the major medical schools through their extensive grants and yearly donations. The main direction of western medicine is drug oriented, not because there is anything inherently superior to it, but because a huge amount of money pours into it and supports it year after year.

No drug company will finance studies and research that fail to strongly encourage drug "solutions" or that encourage alternative solutions to health problems that they do not profit by. Individual people, groups, and especially commercial business ventures do not pay money to support their competition or adversaries.

Imagine if two new board games hit the market (like *Monopoly* or *Clue*), and one group spent nothing on advertising while the second group spent millions over a ten year period on promoting its product. Which group would have the more successful and profitable game? Obviously, the game that had the huge amount of money spent to promote it.

13

Which game might actually be "better" would be meaningless because the money invested in advertising primarily determines which game achieves greater popularity. This is exactly the situation with modern medicine and many other things.

Using various medical journals, media outlets, and the FDA, the modern medical establishment actively attacks, derides and even attempts to eradicate alternative methods (*especially* if these alternative methods ARE effective and would pose a real competitive threat). **Medicine is** *big business***, the only goal is profits, and to hell with whether it works or not.** It's primarily a matter of balance sheets for their respective accounting departments.

Factually, the AMA (American Medical Association) spent over ten years and much time and money ridiculing, attacking, and finding fault with chiropractic practices. They presented it all very "scientifically" with "numerous studies" but often simply resorted to juvenile name-calling in an attempt to belittle the chiropractic profession. Members of the chiropractic profession were often referred to as quacks or side-show elixir salesman. Some of their methods were derided as being nothing but mumbo-jumbo and hocus-pocus.

This is a common practice today. One group attacks another by calling them various things that are known to have unique associated connotations by the majority of the public. "Oh, he's a socialist," "they're atheists," "it's just a cult," and "she's a right-wing extremist" are all examples of where reason, proof and sane arguments are

14

discarded in favor of simple name-calling with the hope that the listener blindly accepts the over-generalized label along with all its unspoken negative connotations. **These planned attacks aim at a pre-conscious and emotional appeal level.** The goal is never to honestly appeal to reason or to discover truth, but to change attitudes and opinions in one's favor.

Eventually, after a long drawn out legal battle, the AMA had to publicly admit and apologize for the dishonest tactics they had used over many years in an attempt to destroy chiropractic. Their apologies appeared in a full-page ad inside *USA Today* **magazine.**

"Truth" and "public health" were not the concern of the AMA or of their cohorts, the FDA (Federal Food & Drug Administration). Their **only** concern was (and still is) profits. The profits of the doctors and drug companies! Chiropractic was competition. It mattered little whether it actually helped people or cured poor health conditions. There is a great deal of information online about the battle between the AMA and chiropractic; simply do searches on Google, MSN or Yahoo for AMA Chiropractic.

Drug advertisements make up the majority of the advertising in all "official" medical journals. The doctors take courses about what drugs to give for what diseases. The drug companies have worked closely with major medical schools for decades to establish the drug approach to modern western medicine.

So, the doctor, whether caring, intelligent, honest or not is basically "educated" (indoctrinated) within a very limited approach to the subject of health.

Alternative subjects, such as chiropractic, homeopathy, acupuncture, and osteopathy, which have been around much longer than modern drug medicine, are routinely ignored and ridiculed by many doctors even though most of them know next to nothing about these subjects.

It is even *popular* to ridicule these subjects. I am sure many wise cracks about these subjects were made at their conventions and social functions. Condescension by people who think they know better when they actually don't is a common albeit somewhat pitiful practice.

Modern western medicine views health as the "absence of disease." They have labeled various physical conditions and packages of symptoms as "illnesses". Their solution is to "attack", "battle" and "destroy" the *symptoms* of the diseases they have "named".

They almost never address an actual cause of a health problem with the aim to solve it. Studies are never conducted to determine how to *prevent* cancer, but only how to *attack* it with drugs and other invasive techniques. The entire intention is to "manage" the pain and to destroy symptoms.

If the illness were truly "solved" this would put their methods out of business.

There is absolutely no profit in curing anything. That is the main reason why they don't.

Many may rebel at this notion and assume that this couldn't possibly be true. The notion violates the basic sense of decency and rightness about the operation of a major social institution. But regardless of intentions, in

16

the real world of existing people and actions, this is *practically* the way it works.

Their intention never has been, and isn't now, to solve cancer. The American Cancer Society, the National Cancer Institute, and the American Medical Association work closely with the drug companies and exist to forward the profits of the drug companies. Otherwise the drug companies wouldn't support them. Many honest and caring people work with and for these groups, believing that they are sincerely searching for a "cure" for cancer. Even many doctors and drug executives believe the same thing, but this is not what they have done in the past, are doing now, or will ever do in the future. One doesn't bite the hand that feeds you (the drug companies). The doctors, colleges and medical associations know this better than anyone, even if this fact is rarely admitted to themselves or others.

Their entire approach isn't to "create health," but to "destroy disease." There is a *large* philosophical difference involved here.

This philosophical gulf results in drastic, practical differences in applications.

For example, osteopathy views "health" as something to *create* through proper diet, nutrition, exercise, and living. It attempts to locate the underlying *causes* which manifest as the "disease" (physical symptoms). Osteopathy might encourage a patient to locate and remove pesticides, food additives, and other chemical poisons from the body's environment and intake, but this is done from a viewpoint of "handling" negative *causes* and not simply "attacking" negative symptoms.

17

It's a major difference in approach and effect. There MUST be *actual reasons* why people develop cancer, but the TRUE sources are not given due concern. The modern popular "authorities" like to assert that it's all due to genetics, so then there is nothing anyone can do about it except pay for their treatments once they have the "disease". It is ludicrous to believe that with all the millions of dollars spent on cancer research that solutions have not been found. This is because the actual causes are not being adequately or honestly looked for.

Research continues to primarily address new ways to attack and destroy *symptoms*, with no aim at discovering actual underlying causes, which if properly addressed would do away with the symptomatic "cures" of surgery, chemotherapy and radiation.

Additionally, there has been a concerted effort by the FDA to attack and destroy any and all efforts that actually do reduce or "cure" cancer. In modern America it is actually against the law to claim that you can "cure" a disease (even if you can).

Antibiotics are a "drug" which helps the body do what it is already trying to do. At the turn of the century, when antibiotics were discovered, great forward leaps were taken in the general health of the public because infections no longer were untreatable.

But most modern "medical" drugs do not act to "help" the body do what it is already doing or trying to do, and, in fact, often act to inhibit or harm the body and what it is trying to do.

Modern drugs, including psychiatric drugs, primarily *attack and suppress symptoms*, rarely addressing or correcting any underlying causes, and almost always with known or unknown harmful side-effects. Even prolonged use of antibiotics has detrimental effects on the body's immune system and other normal body functions. Various proponents of "drugs" try to equate the "antibiotics" with the other newer, modern drugs in their attempt to justify their use. All "drugs" are not equal.

Medical and pharmaceutical specialists want us all to simply think that "drugs are good" and "drugs cure illness." They don't want anyone to have an in depth understanding of what drugs actually do, and that they primarily attack symptoms. Sadly, and for the most part, this is what they themselves believe. Most drugs don't cure anything, and instead almost always *attack symptoms*.

To make matters even worse, most doctors and drug specialists don't even know how or why the various drugs do what they do. Largely they have opinions, notions, and theories which they parade around as "scientific" facts.

They *believe* it, and therefore they can be very convincing. As an example, psychiatrists talk about "chemical imbalances in the brain" as if these actually existed, yet no such imbalance has ever been found in any of many medical studies, and no medical test exists for such an imbalance.

But this *non-existent* imbalance, which has never been detected anywhere at any time, receives constant attention by doctors, is discussed casually in medical journals, and is cited to patients as the "reason" for their problems.

19

It's an illusion, or more to the point, it's a delusion. It's something that many people believe to exist, yet it actually does not exist at all in any way whatsoever. And, of course, the drugs they prescribe supposedly "cure" the invisible and never detected chemical imbalance. It is a hoax. It may not be an intentional hoax, but it is a hoax even if only due to their rampant idiocy.

No two psychiatrists can or will agree on what defines a "schizophrenic" or what the proper treatment should be. The description and explanation of "schizophrenia" has drastically changed over the past century; the concept can mean almost anything or nothing. In a nutshell, the mental illness; the explanation for it, and the cure are all imaginary.

Psychiatry is an often very detailed and complex modern mythology, but it's a mythology nonetheless. These things, such as chemical imbalances in the brain, and many mental diseases are *concepts* which don't relate to any actual, observable realities. These things are fairy tales.

The point is that modern medicine, as it is officially accepted and practiced today, is far from a complete and valid system of health, in theory and in practice.

Doctors are promoted and treated as "professionals," "authorities" and "scientific experts." This is largely a false picture, but has been thoroughly accepted by the majority of the public as being true. Medical doctors enjoy large salaries because they are the primary sales arm for the extremely profitable drug companies.

Make no mistake about it - without the drug companies the medical doctors would not enjoy anywhere near the financial benefits they currently do.

Limited approaches also exist in the fields of psychiatry, psychology, sociology, economics, politics, and education. There are reasons why many modern fields of study are often incomplete, biased, limited, harmful or unworkable (meaning not getting useful effective results), even while the members are viewed at the same time as "professionals" and "authorities."

But in case you are curious, it has mainly to do with profit, power, and elitism (the condition where a certain select few think they know what is best for everyone else due to their self-assumed superior intelligence and ability).

Remember Tom Cruise attacking Matt Lauer during an interview for being "glib" and for not "understanding" the facts about psychiatry? Well, even though Tom may have been correct in his view on psychiatry, his *attitude* very much displayed the common arrogant, elitist, and over-exaggerated sense of "rightness" that Scientologists often exhibit (i.e. "we know the truth, we are the only ones who know the truth, and you don't!).

Do realize that this elitist trait is common amongst people, is not at all limited to the world of Scientology (though this type of elitist view is strongly cultivated within the mind of any Scientologist due to the nature of Hubbard's very effective method of repeated indoctrination), and that such overly obsessive and exaggerated views of self-worth, correctness and legitimacy exist in many areas of life (i.e. fanatical

Muslims, Jehovah's Witnesses, die-hard Communists, and on and on).

Far too many people have this sort of view and attitude, sincerely believing, that he, she or they are the ONLY ones with the truth, and often worse, that it is their firm duty and dedicated goal to foist their beliefs on everyone else.

Fanatics exist in all areas of life; in religion, science, philosophy, politics *and* modern medicine. Be wary of them. Be wary of any and all of them; no matter what form he, she or they take! In a sense, the world can be viewed, examined and understood as an endless parade of various over-indoctrinated hard-core believers (i.e. fanatics) battling each other. "Scientology versus psychiatry" falls quite well within that understanding. You could locate many more such examples if you bothered to take the care and time.

The drug companies and associated non-profit foundations created by the same owners of the major drug companies, dumped billions of dollars into the medical colleges over the past hundred years to support and promulgate their "business". It was all advertising and PR, and sadly, had very little to do with "truth", "effectiveness" or an honest concern for the health of the general public.

The doctor's image as the "kindly", "knowledgeable" and "caring professional" is primarily the result of many decades-long, slick, Madison Avenue type advertising campaigns.

We all believe it, or at least did believe it at some point. We mostly take it for granted, never question it, and this is what keeps the situation going. Mostly they also believe it themselves. It's not that they're really conniving and deceitful, although there are some who fall into that category; but instead they are simply, for the most part, wrongly educated (indoctrinated). Doctor's *are* often kind and caring, but that alone cannot make up for the lack of validity to their approach to human health.

Additionally, the entire nutty system is gaining momentum and continues to expand in terms of influence, power and control. Modern medicine is *not* the result of a hundred years of objective, unbiased research representing Man's honest and legitimate desire to discover "truth" and to "help" solve human suffering. Modern medicine *is* the result of certain huge financial interests that first, aligned themselves with the subject of western medicine, second, refused to support, actively inhibited and even destroyed alternative medical approaches (due to no profit potential and the threat of real competition), and third, completely oversaw, managed and directed the evolution of modern western medicine in theory and practice.

Many people find this difficult to believe, and even completely ridiculous. This shows, not that what I state here is wrong, but that the majority of the public are completely "sold" on the idea of modern medicine as being valid, professional, scientific and all-inclusive.

These people are "modern believers". We all suffer from this to some extent, and none are immune. Any honest and observant investigator will find though that this is simply not true. But you will have to break through much of your own fixed ideas and erroneous basic assumptions

23

about reality before you will be able to see it for what it really is.

It is not easy to admit one has believed a lie for most of their life. This comes as a shock to us all. It makes us feel like fools and idiots. It makes us feel uncertain, unsteady and shaky. Our world seems to collapse around us as the mental props we took for granted yesterday lay in shambles at our feet today.

But it is better to temporarily feel like an idiot, endure the momentary confusion, push through to the other side, and reach a state of increased awareness, than to continue believing and contributing to the lies (modern medicine being *only one example of many*).

The modern doctors *are* "educated authorities", but ONLY within their extremely limited and largely incorrect domain of understanding. Within their own system of ideas or subject they are "smart". They can "diagnose" the "right diseases" by knowing the appropriate packages of symptoms, they can "prescribe" the "right drugs" according to the medical textbooks (which ONLY recommend drug treatments and are written in close affiliation with the major drug companies), and they can discuss "intelligently" their field with other doctors.

The affluent doctors send their kids to medical school, because they have the money and can afford it, new western-oriented medical doctors are produced, and the entire situation continues happily along.

You are familiar with the attitudes about doctors in modern western society such as 1) "being a doctor is a good profession", 2) "doctors are professionals", 3)

24

"modern medicine is the best there is", 4) "medical studies use the latest in scientific methods and equipment", and 5) "listen to your doctor, because he knows best".

It's all largely a sham. While this may not be due to any actual widespread political or financial conspiracy, it is minimally due to ignorance and stupidity regenerating and propagating itself through space and time.

The above things exist only because doctors use drugs.

If doctors, as a profession began to question drug use and began promoting alternative methods to handle patient complaints and ailments, because they honestly found them to be more effective, they would find themselves, as a profession, without a financial guardian angel, because the drug companies would cease to support them.

They would find themselves without power, prestige, and authority, not because they weren't right, but because the *big money* would no longer be setting them up as the "professionals".

Drug companies and therefore the entire medical establishment support drugs and drug use *only*. They do *not* support, and have never supported, "truth", "health" and "honest advancement" no matter what they say, pretend, believe, assert, claim, or promote among themselves or to the public. It is a difficult thing to discover and understand that what we have been taking for granted about a major social institution is largely false.

As an example, most doctors don't have a clue about nutrition and its importance to the smooth operation of the human body. This should seem odd to anyone who

25

honestly considers that good nutrition is a very basic requirement of the healthy operation of any human body.

A human body is made up of atoms, cells, chemicals, minerals, and various structures. The body has numerous different systems, such as digestion, circulation, respiration, lymphatic, immune, and nervous, to name but a few, and these each have unique operations which involve utilizing material from the environment to keep the body going.

The body is a tremendously complex biological machine. There is no man-made thing anywhere that comes even slightly close to it in terms of the sheer amount of systems, relationships of systems, and complexity. Specific body functions monitor and handle sugar levels, electrolyte relations, mineral levels and ratios, blood oxygen levels, cellular toxicity, and *thousands* of other things known not yet discovered or known. Apparently the body keeps itself running and functioning just fine if left to itself and allowed to. This FACT is one thing you will never hear come out of a doctor's mouth that the body's own inherent intelligence operates continually, 24 hours a day, to keep it going, and to keep it going at an optimum level. *It*, whatever "it" is, "knows" what to do at the smallest cellular level right on up to the largest interactive whole body level.

Anyone who cares to observe and learn about the various body functions will be truly amazed at what the physical body does all by itself. The body ingests, assimilates, organizes and utilizes various chemicals, minerals, vitamins, and enzymes as the raw material to keep itself going. Thousands upon thousands of chemical reactions at a cellular and organ level occur in your body each and every second! So, if the chemicals aren't adequately supplied, or if certain of the body's monitoring and organizing functions become impaired due to a past failure to obtain the needed chemicals, it can't remain "healthy". The body needs raw materials such as minerals, water, vitamins, and various chemicals, which it largely gets through food (i.e. nutrition), but also from the air and water. These keep the body machine running and also keep it in good "mechanical" shape. This is common sense, although apparently not to the modern western-oriented medical doctor.

And so many modern doctors pooh-pooh nutritional approaches to health. They sometimes use the notion of the "starry eyed, hippie, health food fanatic" and attempt to attach it to the entire nutritional approach with the purpose of diminishing the public's perception of it as valid and useful.

A generalized caricature of the health-food fanatic is often attached to the various subjects of alternative medicine and used to prevent an accurate perception and understanding of these subjects. Sadly, these tactics work far too often. Too many people accept without question the conceptual associations given to them by others, no matter how untrue or inaccurate these might be.

The modern medical doctors have nothing to do with "creating health". They are only concerned with eradicating or destroying disease, and the removing of disease (which is usually only a group of *symptoms* of some underlying and unrecognized physical problem) is a very incomplete and one-sided approach to the complete subject called "health".

It's not that modern medical techniques don't have their place, they do, but their approach is only an isolated part of a much larger picture. The picture they present of themselves as being the *whole picture* is simply incorrect, and has devastating effects on people, the quality of life and society.

The body is a machine of sorts. It's a biological machine or engine. An automobile engine requires fuel for combustion, oil for lubrication, gas lines to deliver the fuel, oil lines and pumps to circulate the lubricant, a carburetor to monitor and direct the fuel into the combustion chambers, spark plugs to explode the gas, computer systems to monitor speed, oil pressure, gas levels and much more. Nobody questions the importance of using good gas, keeping the engine filled with quality oil, maintaining clean filters, patching leaks or keeping it clean. It's amazing that the human body, which is also a machine, but a *much more complicated machine*, is viewed entirely in a different manner.

Most people take care to ensure their gas is good, clean and free of impurities, yet people eat and drink things everyday filled with toxins which are proven to harm body systems and functioning.

The modern medical doctor often thinks and says that concern for decent nutrition is absurd. It's the doctor who's absurd! He is truly a veritable moron. The surgeon, who is among the highest paid "doctors", excels at cutting out various body tissues with a scalpel, when failure to assist the body in proper operation through decent nutrition, exercise and rest has gone on for so long that it is breaking down horribly. The surgeon is more often than not simply a butcher. That's what he does by

28

definition. He cuts up meat. And society treats him as if he were something special. Again, he cuts up meat like any butcher. Yes, there is a need for this, but no, there is no sensible reason that this should be such a high-paid, well-respected profession compared to others. With a car, any sensible and honest mechanic will look for the *source* of the engine trouble and repair *that*. If automobile mechanics followed the modern medical approach, what follows is an example of what they might do.

Let's say the engine is running uneven (symptom). It actually has a dirty spark plug (another symptom, and a minor secondary cause). The spark plug became dirty because the plug gap was 1) set to small, 2) the gas being used has been cheap (and dirty), and 3) the carburetor was adjusted incorrectly allowing too much oxygen in the fuel mixture causing too much heat in that cylinder.

The "medical" mechanic would aim to handle only the *symptoms* never looking to locate and handle the actual basic causes. He would say, "Oh your cylinder is running funny". Your car has "rough cylinder-itis". The symptom *must* be given a fancy name - this makes it sound so much more convincing. The problem or symptom or condition is viewed *as a thing in itself*, a *disease*, with little concern for actual causes. This *disease* or malfunction must be viewed as something that has a life all of its own, as a unique thing with its own independent and objective existence, with little relationship to anything else, and it is looked at as bad.

He would drill another hole in the cylinder, add a second spark plug to compensate for the poor performance of the first spark plug, rewire the distributor cap, all of which would *cost plenty of money*. This action would weaken the cylinder due to the extra hole drilled in it, opening the door to other problems in the future. The engine *would* run smoother, but unless the faulty spark plug gaps, the dirty gas, and the air-fuel mixture error were located and repaired, similar or *other* symptoms and conditions (i.e. new "diseases") would develop later on. The car might even "appear healthy" for awhile. But 3 or 6 months from now, other problems would develop. Other cylinders would run too hot because the air-fuel mixture was never corrected, and this could "manifest" in new "diseases" such as 1) blackened cylinder walls and corrosive build up which cause the cylinders to experience greatly increased friction ("corrosive-frictional syndrome"), 2) cracked spark plug ceramics ("ceramic dysfunction") , and 3) piston meltdown ("pistonic heat-related failure"). Again, the "medical" auto mechanic would name in excruciating detail and address the conditions or *symptoms* only, making lots more money for himself, the auto shop, and the parts dealers, while still never correcting the actual true *sources of the problem(s)*.

Each of these new mechanical problems would require unique, expensive, but largely superficial solutions, all designed to benefit the "repair industry" and not the consumers. This analogy for the modern medical and the drug industries is *very* appropriate.

The above medical example portrays a specific case of an overall general tendency that exists on this planet in almost any area of modern western civilization. This is the widespread tendency to fail to address true underlying causes, and instead to concentrate only on surface conditions and superficial manifestations.

In other words, true causes are ignored and neglected and *symptoms* **receive the majority of the attention.**

Of course, failing to address the true reasons for anything cannot result in a legitimate repair or improvement of anything, and in a very real sense this is the actual reason for most failures occurring today on an individual, social, national and planetary level.

If you stepped on a nail and the nail became embedded in your foot and caused an infection, you would expect the doctor to remove the nail. You would not expect the doctor to examine the extent of redness and the swelling of the foot, test the infected tissue for the exact type of infection occurring on the foot, clean the area, bandage it, and send you home with a prescription for antibiotics and orders to stay off the foot until it is healed, leaving the embedded nail in your foot. Imagine - the infection keeps recurring because the source of the problem is still embedded in your body. The doctor simply prescribes stronger and stronger antibiotics to control the infection. And when that doesn't solve the infection problem, the doctor puts you on a long-term antibiotic treatment and declares you to be handicapped with a chronic infection that prevents you from walking on your foot. You cannot play sports or engage in other outside activities. In addition, you are exposed to the side-effects of long-term antibiotic drug use, and the underlying problem of the nail in your foot will still be there when they take you off the medication.

A symptom is simply the body's way of letting you know that something is wrong. It's a clue, a red flag. The symptom should not be covered up with a drug.

31

Doing so will keep you from finding out what the body is trying to tell you - what's really wrong.

This is exactly the situation with *modern medicine* - the "human body repair industry". The institutionalized belief system inherent in the modern medical approach pooh-poohs any approach that attempts to address underlying causes instead of symptoms. **Look at aspirin. It handles symptoms. It never actually addresses *why* you have or get headaches, but only suppresses the symptoms.** There are many reasons why you may get headaches, but the medical "professional" cares little about these. Your joints ache, but instead of locating what it is that is causing this to happen, the doctor gives you pain killers to "manage" the pain. *Pain management* is a huge billion dollar a year industry.

Alzheimer patients routinely have extremely high levels of aluminum compounds in their brain nerve tissue. People without the "disease" do not. Instead of trying to discover why and where the aluminum comes from, the doctors give many of them psychiatric drugs to keep them calm, and well-behaved. The drugs "cure" nothing. They suppress symptoms. In the case of aluminum, the primary causes are probably 1) cooking with aluminum pot ware, as it's a fact that cooking in aluminum results in the aluminum "leaching" onto other chemicals and forming toxic chemical compounds, which then get ingested, 2) underarm deodorants which are very high in aluminum compounds, and 3) stomach antacid medications, some of which are very high in aluminum compounds.

I could give pages and pages of examples where symptoms are addressed at the complete exclusion of legitimate underlying causes Again, few people reading such material as this can accept and understand it initially, because they have accepted so much utter nonsense for most of their lives that directly conflicts with the truth here and what they have been led to believe. Who knows what improved levels of health would be available today, if instead of dumping billions of dollars into drug medicine, the money had been invested in researching *actual causes* of unhealthy conditions? But the bottom line is that investing in these alternative approaches did not and does not enable the same degree of profit. So much for the success of pure unadulterated capitalism and the "business ethic" as far as human health is concerned. It is really quite ludicrous that the farce known as modern medicine is viewed as "educated", "professional", and "state-of-the-art". It is an illusion that the entire public largely accepts and believes. It continues to exist *only* because of this *reason* - because the entire public largely accepts and believes it to be true. *Big money* keeps the belief structure intact through general public education, government support actions, television, radio, magazines, books, medical associations, and university level medical education. The information you get from the environment around you tends to be the information you believe, especially when it also tends to be the only information available.

The *reality* of "modern medicine" is a contrived fantasy, an illusion, and a false view parading as "truth". Sadly, this is also true for many other areas of "modern" civilization and society.

Attacking the Negative, Eradicating the Undesirable

I will make a small digression here because this is paramount to a better understanding of what is going on in today's world.

Most major subjects or fields today do not involve the *creation* **of any** *positive* **thing, but almost always** *attack,* *destroy, annihilate* **or** *inhibit* **negative things as solutions to their respective problems.**

This is a key and basic tendency applied in almost all areas of modern activity. It is also a key tendency throughout human history. It is a basic, largely unconscious, approach most people and groups use to address "problems" today. A few examples are:

1) Governments largely do not concern themselves with *creating* or *building* an honest, productive workable society, but instead they concern themselves with *attacking crime, handling dissidents, catching tax evaders,* or *inhibiting disorder.* This is their usual solution to bringing about *peace* and *order* (both dumb goals in themselves but typical for the modern social planners).

It generally involves stopping *bad* **things from occurring instead of encouraging** *good* **things to exist. This mindset falsely imagines that if one were to take away all the** *bad,* **then** *good* **would naturally be left. This isn't the way it is and it never will be that way. The only good and decent things that exist anywhere exist only because somebody at some time** *actively created these things.*

2) The military is *always* used to stop, control or destroy *enemies.* How any military functions is the epitome of

34

this tendency. **Police,** as an activity that concentrates also on stopping or eradicating what it perceives to be bad or unwanted, also functions primarily in this way. **Modern medicine** views disease in the much the same way. It views the symptoms as enemies, and either cuts them out or drugs them into submission. Cancer treatments all brutally attack the cancer, and often leave the immune system very weakened or destroyed. Many cancer patients, having received modern *official* cancer treatments eventually succumb to pneumonia because their immune system is so horribly weakened from the attacks on their body from the cancer treatments. Modern *official* cancer treatments attack the entire biological organism, with the hope that the cancer dies before the patient. A better treatment, or at least a necessary additional approach, would be to also effectively rebuild and strengthen the immune system. That is often what alternative approaches propose, yet they are often ridiculed by the medical establishment. Again, the cancer industry is big business, largely involving major drug companies.

A capable government, with decency, understanding and an ability to communicate honesty (which doesn't exist anywhere on Earth now), would discuss problems with its neighbors, with a desire to isolate true *sources* of their conflicts. Then they would address the *actual sources* and resolve the true underlying *causes* of their conflicts. Obviously, this is an oversimplification, but the point is that *attacking of the negative* or *suppressing the undesirable* is the common modern (and historical) approach to handling international, national, social and individual problems. The aim is almost never to *create a desirable condition*, but to eradicate an unwanted one. It

35

is assumed that removing the negative somehow brings about the positive. But this isn't so. **The positive must be created**. This one-sided approach of attacking the negative has its flaws, and a general unworkability. Destroying and creating are two entirely different things, in theory, in practice, and in results achieved.

Removing immorality doesn't result in morality. Suppressing crime doesn't create a safe society. Removing illness does not necessarily bring about health. Penalizing lack of responsibility doesn't bring about responsibility. *All good things must be created* **as a positive, and not only attacked as a negative.**

But with governments there is also another problem. They often do not want anyone knowing what their true motives are and so are incapable of entering into honest discussions about actual causes. The US government talks endlessly about "spreading democracy", when in fact, the only thing spreading are the major corporations which control the US government. It is impossible for them to enter into honest discussions, because they promote the notion of "democracy" as a cover for their true underlying motives. These true motives are the consolidation and expansion of control by the top major financial powers on the planet.

3) Modern behavior modification techniques exhibit this. The theories and methods aim primarily to spot, name and eradicate unwanted behaviors. Again, any actual sources to the undesirable behavior are largely ignored or invented, and the symptoms (behaviors) are addressed with an aim to get rid of them. Ritalin is given to suppress the hyperactive child's unwanted behaviors, instead of attempting to locate underlying physical or emotional sources that, if corrected, could often handle the unwanted behaviors by allowing the natural *health* and *natural desirable behaviors* to surface.

Factually, many hyperactive symptoms have disappeared in children when their diet or environment has been altered, thereby removing sugar, allergens or chemical toxins.

But to the psychologists, psychiatrists and teachers (who have been educated into these crazy psychiatric notions), it's all "brain illnesses". The drugs act further to harm the child's mind and body. Most psychiatrists dismiss nutritional approaches as "unscientific" and "absurd". This is true stupidity and extreme one-sidedness parading itself as "educated", "intelligent" and "professional". While they may be "educated", they are, in fact total idiots. They are truly stupid people. Allowing them to exist as "professionals" is a burden we all must bear, because the only true thing they excel at is harming people, their minds and society. Their "intelligence" is a complete farce. That many of us has been suckered into accepting their ideas, and also hold the same beliefs and attitudes makes this no less true.

4) Psychiatry demonstrates this quite clearly. Psychiatrists name and label numerous "conditions" which people experience. Again, these names are "packages of symptoms" of some sort. They then call these packages of symptoms "diseases" or "mental illnesses" (while most of them are NOT). Most of these conditions are problems people have with their own mind and life. Instead of ever trying to locate a *source* for the uncomfortable condition or unwanted symptoms, the psychiatrists "attack" them with surgery (lobotomy), electric shock, or drugs, each of which acts to overwhelm the patient's mind, behavior and condition.

The psychiatric "treatments" actually act to push any true mental and emotional problem sources further into the background, making them much more difficult to address at a later time with a more legitimate approach (such as therapy, counseling, family, support groups, or religion).

Also, a person can and should be responsible for their own mind and emotions. Telling them they have a "disease" which is "not their fault" implies to them first, that they are somehow disabled, and second, that there is nothing they can do except take their drugs or receive their shock treatments. This is all very good for the drug businesses and psychiatrists, but not very good for their patients or society.

5) As an historical example, take the Spanish Inquisition. The Priests and Church wanted "holiness" and "Godliness" to reign throughout the land. Instead of *creating* it through communication and understanding, they instead concentrated upon the *deviations* from "holiness", and *attacked* heresy through extensive arrests, tribunals, court trials, torture and even public murder (burning at the stake, etc.). Of course, it's quite impossible to educate sane and observant people into a crazy belief system, and the only available avenue is oppression and force. There are many similar examples throughout history. Nazi Germany, following popular genetic theories, attempted to perfect Man and bring about the "Ubermensch" (Nietzsche's "superman") by sterilizing people with low IQs, and eradicating "poor human stock".

Again, they didn't try to locate the positive of what makes Man great, and *build upon it*, but instead tried to destroy what they imagined inhibited man's greatness. They basically assumed that if all the bad human traits were removed, then only the good traits would be left. What they completely missed is that the good always must be actively created. They basically had a noble idea with a brutally evil means toward reaching their conceived end.

The above examples are actually all cases of applying *force* against something with the *aim to get rid of it.* The attitude is one of *stomping things out of existence.* Sadly, this is the *status quo* approach on Earth for handling just about anything. This is always less effective and produces less lasting results than the opposite approach - creating or building something positive. Later, more will be said about the use of force to suppress things, and why it occurs.

The above examples exhibit a few of the many ways that Man and his institutions have tended to attack the negative instead of encouraging and bringing about the positive.

Part of the problem here is that things are generally attacked that are *viewed* as or *agreed* to be bad, harmful or evil. Too often the things in themselves are not anything really, and the problem is that certain people fixate on these things to the neglect of creating and maintaining positive things.

Numerous examples can be found in personal relationships involving family, sexuality, jobs and friendship. People chronically point out, criticize and attack what someone does wrong, and too often do little to actually help or bring about the positive condition they seem to insinuate they desire in the other(s). Mommy yells at little Billy for touching things in the store, yet fails to sensibly communicate to him why he should not touch things that are not his own. The husband yells at and beats his wife when caught cheating with a neighbor instead of discussing the problems they each have, how to handle these, and both working towards and becoming people capable of creating a worthwhile relationship and family.

Nothing exists if it is not positively created. Knocking down or destroying unwanted things does not result in the positive thing desired.

This tendency to destroy, as some sort of universal solution to any and all problems, exists in most areas of human involvement. It is largely unsuccessful, produces unanticipated results, and most often ends in failure or worsened situations.

Many more examples, in the past and present, can be easily discovered by any observant person. They are everywhere in abundance.

Chapter 2 - Reality, Belief, and the Mind Section 2

Attention

Whatever has attention placed upon it has a tendency to persist and perpetuate for the person or people placing the attention.

If you place attention on positive things, encourage them, and attempt to build, that which is receiving the attention has a tendency to come about. Conversely, if attention is placed upon the negative such as disease, "mental disorders", crime or immorality, even with the intention to stop it or inhibit it, it tends to also persist and perpetuate, because it is receiving the attention.

This is another reason why attempting to destroy things tends to fail. The attention upon the undesirable thing acts to make it persist. This is an observable fact.

Understanding this requires *looking* and being honest with what one finds through one's own observation. You will never deduce this by "thinking", logic or reasoning.

"Thinking" is primarily playing with concepts in your head, whereas as "looking" is simply observing what is. Of course, most people "think" so much, and "think" so chronically every second of every day, that they are quite incapable of calmly setting anywhere and accurately observing what is sitting there right in front of them.

Materialism, Modernism, and Science

While this previously mentioned situation of indoctrination into any time period's limited and unique set of views does exist for all people, at all places and in all times, it exists in a unique way for the "educated", and especially for the "highly educated" people. This presents an interesting situation where the graduates of the "best" schools are considered to be the smartest, brightest, and end up as leaders of government, medicine and industry, but who also ironically suffer from the greatest inability to break out of whatever the current professional and cultural framework is. True, part of their unwillingness or inability to question their own beliefs stem from the basic profit motive. They benefit financially, personally and socially by believing and practicing what they do. But they also usually *believe* it too. This becomes very important when certain views, ideas and beliefs are incomplete, biased, wrong or harmful to people and society. This situation continues to exist today.

Today the general cultural and professional framework is "humanism", "materialism" and "science". Everybody "believes" it, has been indoctrinated into it, but especially the "elite", "very rich" and "highly educated" endlessly promote it and *adamantly* believe it.

When I say "science" I do not mean the "scientific method", which is an intelligent way to determine the validity of anything. **The word "science" refers here to the various disciplines and fields which have arisen from the purported use of the "scientific method" in the *social sciences* such as psychology, psychiatry, sociology, economics, and politics.**

People have an almost mystical connotation attached to the word "science". It is not dissimilar to the religious feeling of faith. It seems to explain all manner of things to most people, while generally they don't have the slightest understanding of what makes something "scientific" (i.e. based upon the strict application of the scientific method involving proper theorizing, testing, model making, observation of results, adjustment of theories, and so on).

The currently established results of supposed science in the *social sciences* such as psychiatry and sociology, while having very little to do with any honest scientific method and filled with incorrect basic axioms, opinions, and biases, are accepted as part of modern "science", and anything falling outside of their strictly defined domains are viewed as "not science", "quackery", "weird" or plain "wrong".

Smart advertisers attempt to attach the idea of "science" or "scientific" to their products and ad

43

campaigns because they know how most people unconsciously favor anything presented as "scientific" (whether it truly is or isn't).

I will attempt to show that these "modern" ideas and views about reality are not superior to any other worldview that has existed at any time throughout history, despite the arguments of their proponents. This is not an easy thing to do because people generally are quite rigidly "stuck" in their current worldview of reality.

A major characteristic of the people who hold a "worldview" (which we all do in some way and to some degree) is that they are quite unable to view reality from *outside* their clearly defined and meaningful framework.

The person holding the modern worldview *believes* it completely, can look back in history and can easily discuss the errors of past worldviews, but cannot notice that he or she is also just another "believer" in a similar type worldview.

Although differing in content, one's modern worldview functions in exactly the same way as all those they look back upon and correctly criticizes and find fault with.

If you are a college graduate, you are probably thinking that this doesn't apply to you. Actually, this applies to you completely. And this is even truer for the graduates and Ph.D.s of Harvard, Yale, Brown, Princeton, and so on.

Now, if you *are* a graduate of one of these, then you are probably now smirking, and condescendingly thinking to yourself how incorrect I must be.

Please read on, if you have the strength of character, any sense of truth left within you, and the slightest ability to question your own basic views and assumptions about reality.

Ideas versus Reality

The majority of people, especially "intelligent" people, think in terms of unique concepts, specific ideas, and numerous abstractions. That's fine and as it must be. Everything has a name, or a label; things are categorized into types and generics based upon similarities; perceived differences in quality and quantity enables us to keep things separated from each other (at least in our own minds).

Realize this is primarily a "mental" function that we humans as minds *apply* to reality around us, and has little to do with "reality" itself. The world of abstraction, concepts, ideas and meaning exists *only* inside of your mind. It has no independent existence anywhere else.

When you call an actual physical tree a "tree", the word or concept is assumed to "be the tree", but it is not anything of the sort. In fact you know very little about that tree you might be thinking of or looking at. You have no idea of the number of branches, texture of the leaves, color of the buds, depth of the roots, thickness of the bark, operation of mineral nourishment, photosynthesis and so on for a tremendous variety of the trees characteristics and functions. You may have *ideas* about it, but they are vague at best. Even more to the truth, even if I gave you a full day, you would still not "know the tree". You could strip off bark, slice into stems, dig for

45

roots, observe leaves under a magnifying glass, and count spring buds, but in the end, you wouldn't have achieved the goal of truly "knowing that tree". You wouldn't understand the "pattern" or "active agency" which resides in a seed and acts to manifest as the tree and keeps the tree functioning as tree, just as that specific tree and tree type, and nothing else, throughout its life.

We mainly see and experience things, at an often very superficial level, give them and the various relationships among these things "names" or "labels", attach personal meaning and significance to these various things, and happily go about our business.

Most people think in terms of symbols and labels for the objects and relationships between the actual objects of reality. They take the "idea" to be the thing and work mentally with these *concepts* about the things of reality alone, usually paying little attention to how closely these *concepts* or *ideas* accurately relate to actual observable things. These concepts are usually *far from equal* to the actual realities they involve and correspond to. And sadly, most people never actually deal with reality or other people *directly* because they never can get past dealing with their own unique and generally severely limited "ideas about" reality and other people. Do you get the difference? It's a big difference.

People's *ideas about reality* (names, labels, concepts, abstractions), and their own personal meanings (remember my treatise on the "Confusions of Man" in the beginning of this book?) about all these things, have much more to do with what is going on in life than any actual understanding of the true nature of

46

the various things or some supposed "objective reality". Add to this the fact that much of what passes as "knowledge" is intentional or unintentional misinformation, and the entire situation becomes very difficult to confront.

This requires further explanation to adequately get across an idea of just how wide a gulf exists between "things" and the "ideas about things" which all people connect and attach to these things.

Some examples will serve us well.

1) A man recently had an argument with his wife. He is thinking continuously about how rotten she is, how she cheated on him, how she is so uncaring, and what he plans to say to her. He has all these "ideas" going round and round in his head. He never really looks at or understands her. In fact, he never has in the four years he has been with her. He understands and thinks with his "ideas" about her, or how he *conceives* her to be.

True, there is some relationship between what he thinks her to be and what she is and does, but there is also much which is purely of the nature of "ideas" about her that are vague, generalized, exaggerated, and also just incorrect. There is a huge gulf between the two, what she *really* is and what his *ideas* are of her. So when he gets home, he yells and verbally attacks her, and still never looks at or sees "her".

He sees her through his own unique set of ideas of what he conceives her to be and what he imagines she *should* be. It's like his ideas, concepts, beliefs, and notions (i.e. his general viewpoint) act as a *filter* to his perception and experience, only allowing him to see and experience a small aspect of her (which may not even be a true aspect at all). We all have this going on to some degree about everything we live, see and experience.

2) A college student is studying basic electrical circuits. He has read all about "current", "voltage" and "resistance". In a lab experiment he sets up a simple circuit with a battery, some wire, and a resistor (an electrical component which inhibits electrical current flow). When he connects it all together, he takes some readings using a voltmeter, ammeter and ohmmeter. He then sees how the voltage, current and resistance are all related. He smiles with his new understanding of electricity. What is really going on here?

He never "saw" a voltage, or a current or an electrical resistance. He never touched or heard any of these. Even today, nobody *really* knows what electricity is. Theories continue to change, but always, and at any time, these are just theories about phenomena of perception and experience. Some people think we, as a civilization, are moving "forward" and "advancing" the theories about the world around us, are getting "closer and closer to the truth" about electricity, energy and reality. That's wrong. That's totally wrong.

There is rarely any advancement. There is only change and differences in human *concepts and notions* about reality. What there is actually is *just another theory*, and it is no better and no worse. It is simply just an *alternative* mental construct, set of ideas, concepts, or notions. Over the past 6,000 years the entire universe has stayed basically and exactly the same. The *only* change has been *man's ideas about it*. The world here on Earth, including the form of civilization, has changed *only* according to Man's ideas about himself and the world.

The idea about a thing can never and will never be the thing itself! All ideas and concepts must, of necessity, fall short of the thing itself. The only way to truly understand something or to truly know something is to be it, and to be it completely.

Geniuses such as Einstein or DaVinci probably had their moments of "becoming" the object(s) of their contemplation. They, for a moment, saw it all in an instantaneous flash of total understanding, and thereafter spent thousands of hours trying to put into words and communicate to others what they had seen in that brief moment of illumination. Einstein probably **was** *a photon, speeding through space at the speed of light, feeling space bend as he neared large suns, experiencing catastrophic amounts of electrons changing potentials and bursting free as mass converted to energy.*

It is interesting to note that religious mystics undergo the same problem when they attempt to communicate what they experienced when they "became one with the universe", "one with God", or "one with their Self".

Possibly, instead of spending all their time trying to communicate what they saw and experienced, they might better have spent their time teaching others how to gain the ability of "being" other things, relationships and energies at will. Although, most likely few ever realized that this is what occurred in the first place. People could then "understand" by their own personal direct experience. This would solve many problems with communication. Of course, if we could all do that sort of thing all of the time then there would be no use for communication or much of anything else.

3) Maggie is walking home from school thinking about how her Grandma promised to make a cake with her after school today. She imagines getting the eggs, cracking them into a bowl, pouring in the milk, adding the sugar, mixing it all up, pouring it into a mold, and finally placing it in the oven. There is much activity occurring in little Maggie's mind. We all have extensive activity occurring within our minds. For all of us, to some degree, these various thoughts, ideas, notions and imaginings are mostly pale reflections, in vividness, detail and continuity, of past, present or future external realities. Memories are remembered, the present is considered, and the future is decided upon, feared or looked forward to.

Sometimes these are detailed, but more often than not, these are part verbal (i.e. mental talking to oneself using the symbolic labels we each have given everything we find around us) and part faint imagery. All of this is continually parading itself across the landscape of our inner mental space. It is an interesting exercise for anyone to try to spend 10 minutes a day for a week or two attempting to quietly observe, without interfering, the nature and content of one's own mind.

Obviously, what I am discussing here is something different than intellectual mental "concepts" and "abstractions", and falls more under the realm of imagination and fantasy. While this is true, my point is to get the reader to view in another way just how an "idea" or "thing of the mind" is *not* the thing it refers to, and often is of much less quality, quantity, character, detail and vividness than the objects and relationships of external reality the ideas correspond to or are supposed to describe and define. Maggie may not be thinking in words or language at all, and may be simply picturing out the entire anticipated event. This can be totally devoid of conceptualization as an intellectual process of thinking with ideas.

What any human mind *does* do completely though is attach meaning, significance and purpose to everything it finds around itself and involves itself with. *There is no meaning outside of any individual's own creation of it.* **The creation of meaning and the attachment of significance to aspects of one's life, and inner and external reality is a function of a *mind*. Only a *mind* attaches meaning. Meaning doesn't reside *in anything* "out there". It is *bestowed upon* things by conscious thinking entities alone whether the object of the bestowing be one's personal hobby, business, family, friends, club, government, city, county, state, country, investments, goals or religion. This may seem heretical to some who are strongly religious, but even if God, Christ, Buddha or Mohammed is ultimately the most vital and real thing in the universe, this is meaningless unless a specific individual mind considers it to be so. This is the sole purpose of absolute truth; the foundation of man's mind to rest on something that never changes, something that isn't fluid or moving. God, as absolute truth, gives a person the right to look at everything through His mind. Listen...**

*****

The World Speaks! It is a question I ask when I find myself in a defeated place of miscommunication, when I see two parties completely misunderstanding one another, or when I am studying Greek: Is language really worth the trouble? Of course, even in a defeated place, most of us recognize the irony of the question itself. To voice the trouble of communication is still to utilize the form of communication. But if it is difficult to imagine a world without the presence of language, it is altogether sobering to imagine a world without its benefits and joys—a conversation with a friend, the power of the written word, the importance of banter, reasoning, and debate.

I believe it is inherently Christian to recognize the weight of language. The first chapter of the Gospel of John echoes the first pages in all of Scripture—namely, that out of silence the universe was brought to order, for in the beginning was the Word. The Greek word logos means not only "word" but "reason," hastening the notion that there is not only meaning at the heart of all things but there is one who speaks and bestows this meaning. The Christian worldview interprets all of life and time through this medium. We live within a story of words, reason, and meaning in which there is an author telling us what it means to be human, what it means to be here.

The presence of language among us, therefore, is itself a subtle apologetic. That is to say, we speak because there is one who first spoke. There is meaning and order among us because in the beginning was the Word. Author Steve Talbott fluently articulates the significance of a speaking world:

"The intimate relation between the meaning of our words and the meaning we find in the world may be so obvious as to seem almost trivial, yet its implications are so

52

profound as to have mostly escaped the notice of working scientists. If we took the fact of the world's speech seriously—the world speaks!—there would be none of the usual talk about a mechanistic and deterministic science, about a cold, soulless universe, or about an unavoidable conflict between science and the spirit."(1)

The evidence of a speaking world is a wonder the scientist cannot explain away with mechanistic words. But what if language is the gift of a speaking, personal God to persons made in God's image? The world speaks and God listens. Will we, in turn, stop and take notice of the God who spoke first?

Into a world of souls, some listening, others preoccupied, Jesus speaks in words common to all: "Here I am! I stand at the door and knock. If anyone hears my voice and opens the door, I will come in" (Revelation 3:20). To recognize a voice speaking in a language we understand is so much more than acknowledging a string of inanimate, recognizable words. We recognize a person beyond the sounds, meaning within the language, an invitation in the face that somehow looks to ours even now. How much more so this is true of the voice that first spoke into the silence and called the world forth by name. - Jill Carattini

*****

Meaning is created and given to things by Man alone. Only conscious, aware beings do this. Attaching or bestowing meaning is a function of consciousness. It is a function of an aware mind. It is *not* a physical or biological process. Human beings should learn to begin paying attention to what he or she believes in, and attaches purpose and meaning to. It is not all accidental, fixed, environmentally determined or a matter of natural personal genetics or social evolution. We each have a choice and it is our own complete personal decision alone what we decide is important, and should receive our meaning and purpose.

The idea of "values", what we each value as important, valid, desirable, right and wrong, comes into play here, and the *establishing and maintaining of values* is another function of a mind. Ideally, one's choice of meaning and value is a conscious and self-determined activity. This is often difficult though, because there are so many forces about us attempting to sell us on their own unique set of beliefs, purposes, meaning, values and opinions without taking into consideration the individual's need to assign value and worth as he/she sees it.

Also, there are only a limited number of *pre-packaged* belief systems (interconnecting and reasonably consistent systems of meaning, belief and concepts) generally available for the public's acceptance at any time and place within any extant reality (such as any fixed location on Earth).

4) Exercise 1: Purpose: To get a "feel for", direct experience of, or awareness of the difference between *being or knowing* something and *thinking or knowing about* it with concepts and ideas.

Details: Choose any simple object such as a glass, cup, key, wrench, cigarette, etc. You can choose anything but keep it fairly simple and small. Look at it for a few seconds. Consider its size, shape, color, weight, location and texture. Think about these things. Consider its similarity to other similar objects of the same type. Think about these similarities for a few moments. Consider how

54

it is different from other objects in the area. Think about these things.

Spend a few moments thinking about how your "ideas" about it are actually ideas only and not the thing itself.

Now, simply sit there, look at the object, and perceive it. Allow it to fill your attention. Wallow in it to the exclusion of all else. Just look at it. See it. Perceive it. If thoughts intrude upon your awareness, either thoughts about the object or entirely different thoughts, gently stop them by withdrawing your contribution to the thoughts. Don't resist, fight or try to force the thoughts to stop. Comfortably cease having the thoughts and continue to be there with the object. Allow the object to pervade your attention to the exclusion of all else. Perceiving, observing and looking are very different from thinking and conceptualizing.

If you do this for awhile, or even for a number of days in a row, you will come to have a better understanding of the difference between "ideas about things" and the actual "things". There is a *huge* difference. You won't ever truly understand this through talking about it, thinking about it, or imagining about it. Only *direct personal experience* can supply the awareness of the difference. In this exercise you must use your *attention* and *awareness*, both sadly under used commodities, and not your ability to *think* or *conceptualize*. These are very different things.

There is a limitation with all words, concepts, discussions, book reading, and intellectual endeavors. While these do all have their place and purpose, and we couldn't really get along without them, these do not and cannot ever impart complete understanding of anything.

55

If the reading, thinking or discussing doesn't encourage and prompt you to *look* and *perceive* actualities out in the world around you or in your inner world, then they are really useless. While this *is* completely true, it is not taught, much less even mentioned in a practical way, within the confines of what passes as "modern education".

"Reason" and "thinking" reign supreme in official modern academia. These two things are only *parts* of any mind, and *lower* in function than awareness, knowing and looking. *Reason* and *thinking* both involve concepts and ideas only. It largely involves playing with *significances about things*, with the thinker rarely realizing that the concepts and ideas never are or can equal the things they supposedly refer to. The concepts and ideas can approach the thing or relationship they refer to, but for most people, most of the time, the gulf between the two is tremendous.

Any philosophy student, or professor, would gain much by honestly doing these exercises, as he would come to a better personal understanding of the difference between *thought* and *reality*, and their relationship. Numerous philosophy courses, book learning, and intellectual gymnastics cannot supplant direct experience. The intellect has its value and use, and it is beneficial to exercise the *intellectual muscle*. Subjects such as logic, mathematics and philosophy are great for this, but most people involved in these subjects take them much too seriously, and don't realize they are simply playing mental games with words, significance and meaning. Most philosophers forever remain *mental* and *intellectual*, and never figure out or know there are ways

56

to directly experience all they argue about and pontificate over. Of course, if they did this they would all be out of a job. No one would take them seriously, and considering the results of most *modern philosophy* this would probably not be such a serious loss.

Advertising executives are constantly attempting to alter a consumer's perception of their products. Reality of the product means nothing to them. Perception through 'experiencing the product" is the ultimate goal. This is why most advertising is directed toward women. Women employ their psyche mostly through experiential filters. Men live life; women experience it! Here is an example:

A woman will shop for perfume – let's say Chanel No.5 – and notice the price tag for 2.5 ounces is $86.00. She won't pay this price because she knows that you cannot patent a scent so she will buy the knock off Chanel No. 5 without the fancy bottle and packaging for $19.95. A man will never buy the knock off because his purpose is different. He knows full well that the knock off is the same as the original, as does the women; however his purpose in buying it is a gift to a woman and would never allow his pride to give a knock off as a gift. The two perfumes are literally the same thing. But each gender views its perception and reality differently.

Exercise 2: Purpose: To get a further distinction between mental *ideas* and *actual things*.

Details: Choose a sign with a written word on it, or write a word on a piece of paper. Do the same exercise as explained above. When you reach a point where you cease to *see* any meaning to the words and the letters themselves become nonsensical forms, then you have achieved an experience of the thing *separate* from your own ideas, significances and notions you have attached to it.

Notice that initially when you look at a word or a sign, the interpretation occurs *instantly AS YOU PERCEIVE IT and not necessarily how others perceive the same word.* You may mentally speak the word in your mind or *perceive* it automatically with whatever meaning the letters or symbol has for you. You do this with *everything* around you and this involves an incredible number of associations between *things* and your own *personal definitions, meaning and significances relating to these things.*

If you do this exercise until completion as described, you will have a very good idea of just how much your own ideas contribute to reality, and how little is actually there by itself. This may take 10 minutes, an hour, weeks or months. If you say, "it didn't work", it only means that you failed to do it until it did.

Those of you who are more *intellectual,* worship *reason,* and tend toward rigid conceptualizing will have a harder time at this. Reason, intellect, and conceptualizing *are* necessary, vital, and useful, but they are only *part* of a much larger picture of what a human mind does and is capable of. Too often, the products of reason are assumed to be all there is. **Reason applied to a detailed examination of the physical universe gave us materialism.** It's only a partial understanding utilizing only a partial aspect of any mind.

If you continued down this path, with methods and techniques I haven't the time to delineate, you could

probably reach a point where you could recognize and completely experience how *all* **reality, as you experience it, in every way, is** *completely and only dependent* **on your own viewpoint, notions, and convictions about it. This wouldn't be an idea, or concept, but a practical experience. It would be above the intellect, actual, true, and not hallucination or imagination. It would probably be termed** *mystical,* **but actually is simply the case of you being there without all one's own personal mental associations about everything you see, have seen and will see.**

This is the goal of certain techniques of meditation although even these subjects themselves often err by attaching themselves theoretically to ideas of God or cosmic consciousness. This *can* result in a tremendous personal experience of awe, clarity, expansiveness and understanding. But there is really nothing *mystical* about it. You would have just suddenly found yourself in direct communication with things without any attached personal meaning or significance to or about these things. This can include your experience of a small pebble, a stick, a leaf, a sun or the physical universe from one end to the other. It can also include the experience of your own mind, awareness, or consciousness separate from all objects and associations with the objects of usual experience. **Any*thing* can be the object of such direct experience or awareness.**

The goal is not to forever destroy all meaning and significance in one's life. This has often been the approach of various Eastern religions, to deny self completely and all one's personal *mental* involvement with all inner and outer reality. But doing this *can* be very therapeutic and can deliver to one a firsthand experience and knowledge of **how large a part each person's individual mind plays in the creation and experience of their own personal life and perception of reality.** The aim is to enable personal control over one's own mental activity, a control that is all but non-existent today and has been for the majority of people throughout human history.

5) Ask most people the question, "why do things fall to the ground?", and they respond, "because of gravity". But ask them, "what does gravity mean?", and they tell you, "Well, the law that things fall".

The word "gravity" *means*, to most people, "things fall to the ground when released from a higher position". The label or term "gravity" is defined as meaning, "things fall to the ground". FACT: *Things fall to the ground because things fall to the ground.*

That's really the understanding, derived from direct personal experience, most people have. Gravity has the definition of "things fall to the ground".

The "label" gravity imparts a sense of understanding to many people, which is quite non-existent. People think that making up some invisible force called gravity sufficiently explains why things fall to the ground.

To this day nobody anywhere has the slightest clue why things fall. The truth, based upon perception, is that things fall. All else is make believe; theorizing and cute games of imagination. People can even talk about this, thinking they actually are discussing something.

In fact, they are only playing with words and meanings. Do you see? The truth is that we each experience things falling to the ground. That is what we truly KNOW.

60

But any explanation or understanding is largely and primarily only in our minds. It's a *concept* of something which really explains and perceives little except what we already directly experience - things fall when dropped. *Concepts* and the *actual realities they relate to* are rarely equivalent, and more often than not, are quite different.

The educated scientist will argue, "But the real theory of gravity involves mass and the attraction power of large masses". Maybe he will also someday figure out that however advanced his notions, ultimately it is only an "idea" about something he experiences. There is a true reason why gravity exists, and why everything else exists as it does. I discuss this in detail below.

There are many concepts we all hold about all types of things which actually are only *definitions*, yet we each believe ourselves to possess "understanding" because we have "named", "labeled" and "defined" something.

In the middle of December in New York City someone says "it's cold today", and a friend responds, "of course it is, it's winter". They each think they "understand" something. Winter is *defined* as a time when it's cold. Of course it's cold!

Billy falls off his bike and hurts his knees. His mother explains, "Oh you just had an accident", and both Billy and his mother feel better.

But "accident" *means* having something happen which you didn't plan which usually has bad results. Again, it's talking and thinking in circles about nothing. And we even get emotional responses from this mental and verbal charade!

A man robs the corner store and a group of people discuss how "he is just a criminal". They all "understand". But a "thief" is by *definition* a criminal. Where's the actual explanation or understanding? I could give hundreds of examples. Life is riddled with this type "thinking". There *can* be more in depth understanding of causes, but this is rarely the case. It tends to be very superficial, incomplete and largely arbitrary regarding any individual's dealing with the objects (or concepts) of life and reality.

6) Racist, oppressive religious activities and domineering nationalistic movements all suffer dramatically from these same problems where reality has little to do with what the members of these groups think about it. The bigot sees thieves in every black person. He never correctly sees that black people, like any people, have the same usual goals as anyone else - happiness, success, peace of mind, love and respect.

"Mind" has no color except as it considers color to exist as a thing of importance. The bigot uses all types of "logic", theories and rationalizing to make "his case" against other races. It is all just so much arbitrary conceptualizing, most of which has nothing to do with observable facts. The Inquisition Priest believes in God, Satan, demons, possession, witches, and all sorts of ideas. He is convinced he is right, and he is going to ensure everyone else follows exactly what he demands. So he declares the heretics, has them tortured or murdered, "saves souls", and even "feels wonderful" about the great job he is doing cleansing the world of unrepentant sinners. He believes this and so did many others. At the time most people were incapable of "seeing outside of" their current social, religious and cultural framework.

Nazi Germany, about 50 years ago, convinced a large population of a major "educated" European country that Aryans were superior, that certain others were inferior, that it was their duty and right to bring forth the "Ubermensch" (superman), and murdered millions of people in the process. Ironically, much of the German psychiatric theories of genetics, eugenics, and heredity, which provided a good part of the Nazi ideological basis for genocide, exist in modern times under the guise of modern psychiatry. They are also now again leading to human oppression, but in a different and veiled manner. People always think they are right, and that they themselves, as part of the "modern world", possess the correct worldview, and are immune to deception and the propagation of faulty views and beliefs. If they don't consciously think this, they at least *unconsciously* take it for granted. But it *is* occurring now, and it's also just as true, as in the past, that a majority of the ideas believed and promulgated are equally flawed and destructive. This modern view exists under the name "materialism" generally, and under the names psychiatry and modern psychology specifically as relates to Man and his capabilities.

There is MUCH to any person's ideas and understandings that follow this same pattern. Words, labels and ideas about things impart a false sense of understanding, making an otherwise complex universe appear somewhat ordered and sensible. We do it to the world around us - it doesn't do it to us.

We each have quaint notions, over-simplistic ideas, and exceedingly generalized concepts, which we place upon everything we see and experience. I should give more examples of this because most people have a real difficult

63

time recognizing how and where they do this, and that they do it so often and chronically. But I will leave it up to you to take a look and discover for yourself where your own ideas have much more to do with arbitrary notions than with any actual objective reality. This isn't necessarily bad, although a casual examination of human history provides many examples of where the results have been bad. Once you realize that it's pretty much arbitrary what you decide to think and believe, will be daring, and choose wonderful and great ideas to forward and relay to the rest of the world (vision). And don't accept the mediocre trash that passes daily through the hallowed halls of official academia and the mass media. Dare to break free of the current mold - it's a stiflingly rigid and lifeless mold. Of course, also realize if you choose notions which others can't relate to at all, that they will place you outside of "normal reality" and consider you crazy or at least very eccentric. People react in funny ways when you believe things they can't get any handle on. Your best bet is to loosen them up a little so they won't react so badly every time they encounter different ideas and beliefs from their own.

The current world is characterized by a glaringly obvious inability to tolerate different or competitive convictions and beliefs in others. _Everybody is frantically trying to sell something to everyone else._ Many believe their own notions to be superior, and that everyone else should also hold the same beliefs. This is an interesting gauge of the planet's level of "spiritual or mental progress". The "higher" or more "advanced" a person or planet gets, the less they or it cares what others think and believe, and the less interest they or it has in demanding that others

64

conform to their own unique ideas, whether these be religious, political, social or otherwise.

This is also a general measure of "sanity". The universe stays pretty much the same within the framework of human life, and human history, and the only real variations which exist, and which also explain every situation at any time throughout human history, are the variations in individual and group *ideas, notions and beliefs*. It isn't simply Man's own strongly held beliefs and convictions, about everything and anything, which make the world what it is although my premise so far is that this is true as it relates to each individual's existence. It is also due to love and God, not to mention the opposing forces of everything that is good...we call it EVIL.

Becoming aware of this inner world of ideas and beliefs, gaining some personal control over it, and encouraging others to do the same would benefit us all. It would strip various manipulators of their power to manage and control mass belief, because more of us would be aware of how belief works - its formation, acceptance, change and destruction. For too long Man's inner beliefs have been controlled by external forces, either by accident or by purposeful design. It's time for Man to begin controlling his own beliefs and convictions himself. You will have beliefs and convictions regardless; why not take some control and responsibility for them? But doing that *first* requires a good understanding of the mind and the nature of beliefs and conviction.

Chapter 3 – Reality, Belief and the Mundane Section 3

Reality - Gradients of Belief

You might believe the Beatles to be the best band of all time, you know it, and so you experience it. You believe you love your wife and so you do. You believe in modern science and so you experience all its wonders. You believe in modern psychiatry and thus conceive yourself to suffer from manic-depression, suicidal ideation or a chemical brain imbalance. Similarly, and in exactly the same way, although it's much deeper and currently beyond your own personal awareness and control, you believe the entire physical universe to be "out there" just as it is with all its laws and time and space, and so it is for you. And so it is for everybody.

People make the mistake of thinking conviction follows experience (seeing is believing). **This is only an illusion. They think they live, experience things and *then* develop ideas about what they experience. This only appears to be true. Actually, experience *follows* conviction and rigid belief, always and in every case (believing is seeing). This is true regarding your own personal experiences of day to day life, as described above, but also applies to anything from your experience of a galaxy right down to the smallest atom. What makes the "external universe" so imposing is that we all, together and in a very similar way, mutually hold the same convictions about this thing we experience called the physical universe. Billions upon billions of conscious entities (i.e. people) are contributing to the notion that it exists and how it exists.**

You know when you really feel something is true (subjective truth), whether this be an idea about a friend, a movie, a book, an author, a car, a job, a hobby, or anything. But you also know that you can look back and wonder how you could have ever possibly believed certain things, yet these things were completely "real" to you at some past point. Things are subjectively "real" when you *believe* they are real, or when you *agree* with them to be so. This is what subjective truth is all about – it appears real but is subject to change. They are "real" to you, are "true" for you, and "exist" for you. For all practical purposes, these three words mean the same thing in

personal experience. But they are all based and dependent upon belief.

*****

The New Atheism - Though the chorus of voices decrying belief in God has been humming in the ideological background for centuries, it seems to have reached a crescendo with the emergence of a movement that has been dubbed the new atheism. The trademark of this new brand of atheism is its vitriolic attack on religion. To its advocates, religious beliefs are not only false; they are also dangerous and must be expunged from all corners of society. The pundits of the new atheism are not content to nail discussion theses on the door of religion; they are also busy delivering eviction notices to the allegedly atavistic elements of an otherwise seamlessly progressive atheistic evolution of Homo Sapiens.

Given the rhetoric, one might be forgiven for thinking that some new discoveries have rendered belief in God untenable. Curiously, this drama is unfolding in the same era in which perhaps the world's leading defender of atheism, Antony Flew, has declared that recent scientific discoveries point to the fact that this world cannot be understood apart from the work of God as its Creator. This is no small matter, for Flew has been preaching atheism for as long as Billy Graham has been preaching the gospel. Unlike Flew and others, the new atheists seem to forget that the success of their mission hinges solely on the strength and veracity of the reasons they give for repudiating religion. Venom and ridicule may carry the day in an age of sensationalistic sound bites, but false beliefs will eventually bounce off the hard, cold, unyielding wall of reality.

68

A good example of a claim against religion that does not sit well with the facts of reality is issued in the form of a challenge to the believer to "name one ethical statement made, or one ethical action performed, by a believer that could not have been uttered or done by a nonbeliever."(1) We are expected to agree that no such action or statement exists, and then conclude that morality does not depend on God. The problem is that the conclusion does not follow from the premise. The fact that a non-believer can utter moral statements and even act morally does not logically lead to the conclusion that morality does not depend on God, much less that God does not exist. This challenge misunderstands the believer's position on the relationship between morality and God.

The believer's claim is that the world owes its existence to a moral God. All human beings are moral agents created in God's image and are expected to recognize right from wrong because they all reflect God's moral character. The fact that human beings are the kinds of creatures that can recognize the moral imperatives that are part of the very fabric of the universe argues strongly against naturalism. Unlike the laws of nature, which even inanimate objects obey, moral imperatives appeal to our will and invite us to make real decisions on real moral issues. The only other parallel experience we have of dos and don'ts comes from minds. Thus when the atheist rejects God while insisting on the validity of morality, he is merely rejecting the cause while clinging to the effect.

Without God, morality is reduced to whatever mode of behavior human beings agree on. There is no action that is objectively right or wrong. Rape, hate, murder and other such acts are only wrong because they have been deemed to be so in the course of human evolution. Had human evolution taken a different course, these acts might well have been the valued elements of our moral code. Even Nazi morality would be right had the Nazis succeeded in their quest for world dominance. Unless the world contains behavioral guidelines that transcend human decisions, there is no reason why anyone should object to such conclusions.

Though some religious people do not live up to the moral principles they prescribe, it is not true that genuine religious devotion makes no difference to one's moral commitments. It is missionaries, and not atheists, who regularly give up their own comforts and accept unbelievable amounts of pain and suffering to better the lives of societal outcasts, not just through preaching but also through education, technology, and humanitarian relief. Our failure to live up to what we know to be right provides empirical evidence for the need for God's intervention in our lives.

Those who insist that objective morality makes no difference to human autonomy still expect morality to guide the behavior of others. That our society is saturated with transcendent moral sentiments accounts for the popularity of some television programs that arrest our attention night after night. Perhaps ninety percent of the shows they contain depend exclusively on our ability to apply objective moral standards to the actions of the characters. Should the Judeo-Christian moral bank close its doors to our cultural psyche, the bankruptcy of human-centered morality would eventually send our spiritual tentacles scouring for an alternative transcendent anchor. Thus were the new atheists to succeed in their quest, the result would not be the elimination of religion but the entrenchment of a different religion. As Ravi Zacharias has warned, eventually, the real choice for the West will not be between Christianity and atheism but between Christianity and some other religion. Beware of ethical naturalists bearing moral gifts. - J.M. Njoroge

*****

Most of us can understand this. What most of us can't understand, and even less experience directly, is that *anything* "real", including the entirety and specifics of the physical universe, is experienced as real *only* because it is believed in, held with unwavering conviction and agreed to be so.

The thing which makes something "real" to any person is his degree of belief, acceptance, agreement or conviction in it. In other words, when it becomes a belief system in the subconscious mind it is real to that person whether it is subjective truth or absolute truth!!

Whether this relates to an opinion about something, an idea, *or* the physical universe itself is just a difference in *what* is believed in. The unifying principle common to all realities, whether "external" or "internal," is that they exist to the degree with which they are believed to exist!

To a Mets baseball fan they are the most real team. He's committed to the notion that they are the "best" (whether they win or not), and he is familiar with the team members and agrees with information about each of them. He can argue with fans of other teams all day long. He believes them to be the best, he "sees" them as the best, he "perceives" them as the best, and he experiences them as the best. Believing, perceiving, and experiencing occur almost simultaneously.

Perception is not really "seeing what is", but seeing what you "believe to be".

This is "reality" to him because he agrees with and believes it. The Mets are more real to most people than some small minor league team. The minor league team exists just as much as the major league teams, has a similar number of team members, follows the same rules, and plays almost the same number of games per season, but it is not as "real" as the major league team.

First, many people simply aren't aware that they even exist.

Second, fewer people have beliefs and notions about minor league teams to the same extent as they do about major league teams.

What makes something more "real", is 1) agreement that it exists, and 2) the more people who consider it to exist in a similar way.

The Catholic Church is more real to most people than, let's say, Hari Krishnas. Catholicism has more "thereness" than the Hare Krishnas. You might say, "That's because the Catholic Church has numerous churches, priests, activities and influence". This is true, but these things are true *only* because more people agree with the ideas about the Catholic Church and *contribute* to the idea of the Catholic Church. Without *that*, there would not be more churches, priests, activities or influence.

The existence and reality of anything depends upon 1) agreeing with it, that it's "there" and that it possesses certain qualities and attributes and 2) the quantity of people agreeing with it.

There is nothing you experience which falls outside of these requirements. As an exercise, choose two or three things that are real to you and write out 1) what your concepts are about this thing, and 2) how many people agree with the same thing.

Notice that the things which more people agree with seem to have a more lasting and "objective" reality to them even though they may be subjective truth.

Do the same exercise for two or three things which others consider to be real, but which you don't fully agree with. You will notice the same things.

You *could* imagine (fantasize) something as real which nobody else does anywhere. It would be real for you and you would experience it to some degree. As reality gets more "there", and "objective" (objective to you but really subjective), more people join into the co-agreement with the idea, and observable things take form which you experience as separate from yourself. But it's all only a matter of degree. That which seems the most "there" and enjoys the greatest "objective existence" simply has the most unwavering belief about it by the most people (minds) - this is, of course, the physical universe.

Some people consider Elvis Presley to be the best rock 'n roll ever produced. It's not that's it's true or false, only that more people consider it so, than let's say, the idea that the Electric Prunes (a garage band from the 60's) are the best band or rock act.

Truth is what is considered to be true, for the most part (this is subjective truth). It has very little to do with any "ultimate" or "necessarily accurate" truth (this is still subjective truth unless the truth is unchangeable (this is objective truth).

It is actually quite arbitrary. Any "real" basic truth would involve the nature of minds and how they create reality through their own beliefs, convictions and agreements. All else is pretty much temporary and arbitrary. The true source, the ultimate reality, is "in here" (objective and never changes) and not "out there" (subjective and susceptible to change). "Out there" exists only because you believe it does - and this belief is so strong, impervious to change, and has been held for so very long that it is near impossible to understand how this can be so.

You, as a mind, and what you do to create "reality" is not necessarily true reality but perceived reality and for most people this is about the closest you will ever get to an absolute truth.

You can change your ideas about many opinions, but less so about things you *really* are convinced of or are highly committed to as beliefs. The more you believe, the more you are convinced, and the more "real" it is for you - the more you *experience* it as "real" - the more it seems to "exist". Also, the more you believe and are convinced, the more you believe the reality to exist independently of your own notions about it (which isn't true at all). Your experience of the physical universe is an extreme case of belief and conviction, where you are incapable of altering

74

your agreement with it at will. You believe it to exist entirely independent of your own notions about it. The phenomena of the physical universe are just an extreme example, at one end of an extensive panoramic gradient scale of belief and conviction possibilities.

Simply, the physical universe and all its laws, time and space, exists because *you believe it exists*. It has no absolute existence outside yourself (for you). This is true for anything you experience.

What the scientist and philosopher are "discovering" are the basic agreements, beliefs and convictions each person unconsciously holds about it all.

Belief, conviction, and agreement are necessary for *any* reality to exist and be experienced, whether the "coolness" of one's Porsche, the "care" of one's mother, the "idealism" of youth, the "beauty" of a statue, the "honesty" of a friend, or the "genius" of a philosopher.

With the Porsche, most of us can understand what is said here, because many of us don't care at all about or recognize the "coolness" about it. And for those of us who consider a Porsche to be the "greatest" car, we can usually accept that our notion is more of the nature of "an opinion" and has little to do with any inherent "coolness" in the Porsche. The "coolness" isn't there waiting to be discovered - certain of us simply consider it "cool". And those of us who do consider this truly experience the "coolness" when we see one. Yes, there is *something* about the Porsche which elicits this. The style, shape, contours of the lines, and fine engineering. But the concept of *style* is wrapped up in so many notions and personal conceptual proclivities, which act as "beliefs" of

75

a sort. Without your notion of something like style, there would be nothing to give this name to. The same is true for the notions of shape, contour and engineering.

Without you *first* believing, agreeing, or considering *these* also to exist, they would not and could not exist. This can be taken further and further back along a trail of underlying beliefs, convictions and agreements about anything one can experience as reality.

"Style" doesn't exist "out there" anywhere. It's a notion of a mind, which has been *placed* "out there", and when other minds have been taught the same notion, and agree with it, then they can also experience, perceive, and notice it. People say "she has style". She has nothing really, except what you and me first, believe to exist as a thing, quality, or characteristic, and second, then attach this unique significance to regarding specific things and situations. This can be examined and said about anything.

Some will argue, "But my mother does care for me". It exists whether I notice it or not. True, but *first*, both you and her had to have a clear notion of what "care" and specifically a "mother's care" meant before either she could exhibit it or you could experience it. It had to be *placed* into existence as a thing, as a possibility, as a package of actions and tendencies, as a notion, before anyone anywhere could exhibit or experience a "mother's care."

Conversely, the "lack of a mother's care" is also defined whatever way someone chooses and this is where people really get "messed up" and requires counseling. Now think...is it possible to believe that your mother did not care for you when just maybe your perception is wrong? Let me give you an

76

example. A patient of mine was an orphan one of his teachers adopted him at 8 years of age. To this day, and he is 45 now, he firmly believes that his birth mother did not care about him and tossed him away like yesterday's garbage. There are no underlying facts to support this perception but it bothered this man so much I ask an investigator friend of mine to find his birth mother. What the investigator found was that his birth mother gave him up for adoption because she was terminally ill and died two months after giving birth to him. When I told him this he had an extremely hard time accepting this TRUTH because he didn't want to accept this truth. He wanted people to feel sorry for him.

You can take the beliefs, agreements, and convictions of existence about anything logically back further and further along a line of some experience until a point is reached where there are no more underlying explanations of belief, agreement, or conviction. At that point it's pretty much like in Genesis of the Bible, where God said "Let there be Light and there was Light".

In the beginning you simply stated something to exist, by fiat alone, or agreed with someone else's original statement of existence of something, and when you made the statement of original existence or agreement with another's statement, so did the thing immediately exist. It is this and this alone, which is the basic actual source of any person's total experience of reality, and of the reality itself.

Of course, our personal experience seems to deny this, but only because we have each traveled for so long down a road of adding to, altering, denying and rearranging previously existing beliefs, agreements and convictions.

It's as if you started with one stick match, built a small hut, added a room, added another, built a second level, changed the size of another, rearranged a few others, brought in one, then 10, then hundreds, then millions of helpers, and continued along this line for billions of years.

You would be hard pressed to recognize the actual development of the now all encompassing and imposing structure. This is a good analogy to what the physical universe now is for each of us. It is also a good analogy to what many other things, which are part of experience, are for each of us.

It has been a long time since anyone made basic or original statements of existence (i.e. postulates, agreements, beliefs, convictions) which then instantly appeared as directly perceivable realities, and we all agree with *already existing* things instead of initiating new and previously non-existent realities. But the already existing realities are based upon *earlier* actions of agreement made by the minds involved with those realities.

Ecc 1:9 Whatever has happened before will happen again. Whatever has been done before will be done again. There is nothing new under the sun.

To take this *all the way back* implies a few things. First, that thinking minds have been involved with this physical universe (ever hear of God?) as long as it has been here (otherwise it wouldn't be here), and second, your own personal notions about all types of things, and there are a

78

very large number of these whether you can verbalize about them or not, have developed over a very long period, not restricted to this lifetime.

You can draw from that what you like.

God and His Word are the only absolute truths in the universe. Everything from man is subjective; however the way the mind works, people ASSIGN objectivity based on how and what they believe in.

In my studies of the mind, it is interesting to witness how people respond to a higher being; an omniscient, omnipresent being that controls everything around them but grants a degree of control to his created beings (us) to a large degree so that we are able to choose how and what we believe and live out our existences within our set of choices both good and bad.

But everything comes with a cost and most of the time people simply don't count the costs of anything they believe in that manifests in their lives because of their beliefs and convictions. Eve was tempted in the Garden of Eden by Satan and he used the phrase, "God knows that when you eat it your eyes will be opened. You'll be like God, knowing good and evil" (Genesis 3:5).

Satan – himself a created being – was cast out of Heaven because of its desire to usurp God and His position as God. All of the above paid a heavy price and Man today is still paying the price corporately.

What many of you have probably surmised as the underlying premises to this book is that yes; we are in control of our beliefs and, yes; we do control what is manifested both good and bad through the operations of our mind; however, although God grants us God-

like powers through our minds we cannot overrule His will nor his physical laws and anything else He chooses to place before us in this world. After all, the Good News was told to people like that, although they are now dead. It was told to them so that they could be judged like humans in their earthly lives and live like God in their spiritual lives.

Other religions cannot fathom these absolute truths and refuse to remove themselves from their God-like positions. Man is constantly elevating himself to God's level while at the same time bringing God down to man's level and this is simply a fallacy of both fact and fiction.

What was true in the examination of the Porsche's "coolness" or a "mother's love" is no less true for one's experience of the physical universe - the "coolness" of snow, the sensation of "velocity", the texture of "roughness", the aroma of "sweetness", the color "red", the feeling of the "sun's warmth", and the perception of the space between where you are and the nearest star all depend upon the same belief, conviction and agreement for them to exist and for you to experience these things. The real difference between "subjective" and "objective" accepted truth is that the former is subject to change while the later is not and never changes.

The more people consider something to be true, the more "reality" it has (but is it subjective or objective reality?).

There is more *quantity* of belief and conviction contributing to it. With the physical universe it is a case of complete and total conviction by all beings participating in it (even though we know very little about the physical universe).

That's why it appears to be so "real", "so solid", and so "objective" because of the fixed belief and unwavering conviction by billions upon billions of beings. That's *why* it's so "real", "there" and "acts as it does". But until science discovers and proves everything about the universe then it is still subjective in nature.

And just as you may now love classical music and not understand how you ever could have enjoyed hard rock music, and you can feel and understand the "illusory" and "arbitrary" nature of realities through this noticeable personal difference between past and present musical tastes, so is even the physical universe basically and ultimately an illusion and arbitrary until proven.

It is a fixed, solid, and very complex "illusion", but it is an illusion nonetheless, deriving its substance from yours and my beliefs alone. It's true because it is adamantly conceived to be as it is. The highest level *truth* is you and your beliefs as a conscious being of objective and unchangeable truth. *All* else is arbitrary and ultimately subject to change and dissolution - including the physical universe and your relationship to it.

The physical universe, in a sense, is an idea which has come to be severely believed, or stated in another way, a complex grouping of concepts which we are each thoroughly convinced about and agree with. Yes there are certain aspects of the universe that have been proven and these aspects are objective. But the majority of the thing we call the universe is still to be discovered and proven into objectivity.

But the underlying fundamental *truth* beneath it all is *you (and ultimately God)* - *everything* else is what you have come to believe about all manner of things.

Reality is based upon what you accept as true, what you believe, and what you assert in a convinced manner. The more rigid the belief, the stronger the conviction, and the greater the degree of acceptance alone determine "how" real it is. There is nothing which falls outside of this mechanism for you or anyone else. In a very exact and strict sense you are the ultimate creator of all you experience - without qualification.

This is what various Eastern religions and philosophies have meant by "all is illusion". It's not that it isn't "there". It *is* there. But it's not *there* in any necessary or ultimate or objective sense unless you believe in the God of the Universe – not Buddha, not Muhammad, and not any other false god.

If it is not there in any absolute or objective manner (from God), it still CAN be there as subjective truth (from you and the surrounding worldview) but never separate and removed from your awareness or consciousness! In fact, it is there for you *only* because of your awareness. This is another of those things which make much more sense when directly experienced.

While many people can understand this about their own and other's opinions and personal likes and dislikes, they fail to allow this idea to apply to the physical universe. They will argue until the end of time that the physical universe is all "objective" reality (which it is) separate and unrelated to their own notions about it (which it isn't).

In fact, the materialist will even begin foaming at the mouth in psychotic fits of rage if you press the point. He

82

is a fanatical *believer in the worldview*. He *agrees* much too strongly with the accepted ways of the world. He is *convinced* beyond all convincing that there is no God. He has all types of "logical" arguments to support his view - but so does any true believer in the worldview and unbeliever in God. Of course it is *real*; he *believes* this more than anything!

The problem is that you think you experience it *first*, and then decide its "objective" and "there without your own involvement" following your experience of it. But as already discussed, reality *follows* belief, and your conviction preceded the experience of it (believing is seeing). Once the physical universe is there for you, you can go on *pretending* you have nothing to do with its reality and maintenance, and that's basically what we all do. Belief and conviction precede reality and its experience. Always! Ultimately, it's only a matter of degree. God created the universe. It is there but unless you believe it is there, you cannot see it. Once you believe in it; you exist within it and manifest things within this framework based on how your mind believes within this framework.

1) You think that (agree with the notion that) your wife is beautiful, and so you experience her to be. This is based upon your own personal agreements with what beauty is to you and nothing else. One person looks at a sunset and experiences huge waves of aesthetic intoxication, whereas 10 other people don't notice it at all.

Is the beauty in the sunset or in your perception of it? It's totally in you. Ever hear the saying, "Beauty is in the eye of the beholder?"

With your wife, you may have believed and experienced almost instantaneously, so you can't easily separate the two, but the *conviction* in what makes something beautiful and that *she* is beautiful did, in fact, precede your *experience* of her as beautiful. Also, if you allowed yourself to be completely aware of your total cause and participation in making the idea, then you couldn't "experience" her beauty with such "force" and impact. You must pretend you have nothing to do with it to be the effect of things (imagination and fantasy).

If you are constantly aware of your own direct participation and cause in what you experience, it tends to lose its "wallop". And with sensation, we all seem to enjoy and desire the "wallop". So we allow ourselves to forget that it's actually our own beliefs, agreements and convictions which really make it all what it is for us.

This notion above describes in detail how our imaginations and fantasies disconnect from our intellects and embrace lust rather than love. Lust is losing its "wallop" and needs to be renewed.

It's hard to feel and experience the wonderful fragrance of a rose when you fully realize you created the sensation in the first place, that the awareness of the fragrance can exist entirely independent of the rose, and that you are responsible for the association of the rose with that fragrance. So again, you choose to allow yourself to ignore your actual cause in it all so you can experience. So it is with everything. Obviously, this ultimately leads to the acceptance of personal responsibility for everything you experience.

This is important: using the two examples above, the way you see your wife's beauty will be different if you

embrace God rather than hold a worldview of beauty. God's defines beauty from the heart; the world embraces outward looks. See the difference? The framework we choose to operate in is most important. Everything else stems from within the framework of God or the worldview. God teaches love; the world teaches lust.

2) A person believes in God, conceives Him to possess all manner of attributes, prays to Him, and experiences His grandeur, all-pervasiveness and eternity. A person's worldview concepts of being, cause, power, eternity, love, and existence are all tied up in their worldview beliefs and can be diametrically opposed to how and what God defines as being, cause, power, eternity, love, and existence. Most people can understand this when they look at other religions but are quite incapable of seeing how this applies to their own, because of necessity, with religion, one must hold the idea that their God exists independently of one's own beliefs for it to have true meaning for them.

But, regardless, the *psychological basis* is the same as anything else - one believes, agrees, is convinced, and thereby experiences the "reality" but in the case of God this reality is objective truth because God doesn't change. In the case of religion, the conviction is stronger, and therefore the reality is more "fixed", and considered to be "objective" and unrelated to one's own ideas about it. In other worlds there also exists gods that are subjective in nature and consequently they are also subject to change. But then it does raise the question of exactly who made who.

3) The physical universe is the logical extreme of this process, where belief and conviction are so strong, that the "reality" truly appears to be completely independent and is also experienced as completely independent. But in actual fact, it is due solely to the same process of conviction preceding experience. It *is* only and completely because you consider it to be so.

The more firmly you are convinced or believe, the more "real" and permanent something appears, and the less you are able to willingly change your opinions about it, because you have given it the power of a "separate existence" through your own extremely rigid and unwavering convictions about it. You have handed the power over to anything which seems to have power over you through your own notions, beliefs, and convictions about it, both good and bad. This, while far from a complete picture, is the true nature of reality and your relationship to it. It is ALL based upon you, and nothing which is for you ever had a source other than your own awareness, thought, belief, conviction and agreement. In effect, you are ultimately responsible for everything you experience, because you are the only one responsible for the creation of your own strict beliefs and convictions. Even objective truth must be accepted by you to become a belief system and even if rejected by you, it is still reality and truth.

Unbelieving Man (he believes in the worldview but not God), through his own deep seated convictions created and creates the entire physical universe moment by moment. Man's mind, and what all minds do, is the true source of anything, good or bad. Materialism has passed the power over into the hands of the *result* of Man's own creation, material reality, while also denying completely Man's primary role and responsibility for everything and anything. The physical universe exists due to Man's ideas about it. It's actually a creation of his own, yet he has bestowed upon this creation an undeserved existence and power over himself. Materialism, as a belief system, has gone so far as to even remove Man and his mind completely from the equation of cause, purpose, and responsibility for anything, including his own life.

In a very real sense the entire physical universe exists as it does for you *only* because of your own unbendable and unconscious convictions about it. There is much more truth "in you" than "out there", and "out there" exists much more because of you than due to any "objective" existence of external reality. That's why all the efforts of scientists and philosophers can seem a bit ludicrous. They are endlessly attempting to tear apart the physical universe or the universe of meaning in an attempt to discover "truth". But in the end, those things only exist "in" you and me by belief in God and not the worldview. Where's the truth then? Some advanced nuclear physicists are coming to the same conclusion as they ignore God in the process.

For Man to experience wonderful and decent things, or to create a sane world, he must have some idea of his own participation in the creation of these things. This requires a basic understanding and application of the idea that Man creates reality and experience through belief and conviction. When Man's mind is denied, and the product of his mind, physical reality, is placed in a senior position, there can only be chaos, confusion and degradation. This is a key result of modern materialism.

Take a painter who paints a glorious masterpiece. He's the creator. The picture is the created. Everyone sees, admires, adores and appreciates the painting. It is obvious, apparent, "out there" and experiencable. The painter's potential, ability, and genius are not directly perceivable except through his painting. For all practical purposes, the "painter" is invisible. People place the painting on an alter. They come and look at it daily. They build a roof over it to protect it from the elements. After 20 years it is seen to be fading, so it is treated with special preservation chemicals. A strong storm damages the frame, and people attempt to repair it. A tornado tears off the roof and others come to patch it up. A bomb tears half of the picture away and others frantically come to locate the pieces and piece it back together. Some few hundred years later many folks still admire, revere and even worship what's left of the original picture, which is now nothing compared to the original. In fact it's a severely weathered, altered, damaged and deteriorated hunk of material held together by tape, nails, paint, adhesives and numerous other mechanisms.

The painter happens by one day and wonders what is going on. He is dumbfounded. He looks at the absurdity setting on the altar. He looks at them and asks, "Why didn't you call me - I would have painted another . . ." The crowd turns away back to their painting and ignores him.

The majority of people are hypnotized by the observable physical reality, by the paintings of painters, and by the creations of creators, and they generally ignore and are incapable of noticing, much less seeing the importance, of the "hidden" painters or creators. The "stuff", the "things", the "observable

physical reality" gets all the attention. In a sense it sucks you in. And you neglect and fail to notice the vital and integral part played by the painters - and we are ALL painters of our own reality and experience. So if you don't like your life or experience of life, paint a new picture. Stop trying to keep alive and sustain an old and worn out painting. Let it go. Just paint another. That's where your true power lies - in your mind - you are ultimately a creator of the highest degree. Reality is what it is for you *because* of you and for no other reason.

Granted, none of us are currently able to willingly change their convictions about the physical universe and have it change or go away as a directly observable personal experience. It is quite all right to conceive the physical universe to be an "objective", self-existing thing, quite separate from your notions about it. The relationship between the physical universe and Man's mind is still of great importance, and the modern materialistic tendency to ignore and oppress Man's mind is occurring regardless of what you understand the physical universe to ultimately be. So, if you found the above confusing, unacceptable, absurd, of to be "bad philosophy", ignore it and disregard it completely. The information here about Man's mind stands complete without any metaphysical meanderings about the nature of the physical universe and your actual relationship to it.

Chapter 4 – Reality, Belief and the Mind Section 4

Acceptance and Belief

Most of what people think, believe and take to be true is derived from second and third-hand information. It is not based upon direct personal experience. Of course, civilization couldn't exist and advance very well if every single human being had to start from scratch and learn everything all over again. It is necessary for past experiences, understandings and knowledge to be **"packaged"** and passed along as ideas and concepts from one generation to the next.

But most people never become aware of the difference between second-hand information and actual experience.

This would be fine if the knowledge, information, conclusions and concepts were always valid, accurate, and useful to humanity. This is not always the case.

People have a natural tendency to accept unquestioningly the concepts and ideas they are given. This simply is the way it seems to be.

Maybe it's because most people are so naturally trusting. Whatever the "reason", this is how people tend to operate with building their ideas about reality.

Ideas can be received through culture, family, discussions, or study. We tend to accept whatever we happen to be presented with by those around us. This is obviously true while one is growing up, but equally true in lower and higher education.

People tend to believe what they see on TV or read in the newspapers. Why? Because *it's there*! It is there and it is saying something. So it is accepted.

There is no reason to assume what appears in the mass media is true, and often it is not true, only partially accurate or distorted in some way. But for some strange reason people tend to believe that everything they are told is 100% accurate, honest, the full story and researched with care.

Manipulators know this and use it to their benefit. They say whatever they want, whether true or false, good or bad, so long as it gets you to think and do what they desire.

They know if something is said and presented with "authority" and an attitude of "this is the way it is" that most people simply accept it.

Factually, the media presents a filtered, edited version of reality at any time - it is often very far from a valid and true presentation of actual facts and events. The *meaning* of these facts and events is almost always altered in some way.

Lastly, the visual media relies largely on presentations with *emotional* impact. Why? Because some folks figured out a long time ago that ideas are accepted much more readily, and without conscious questioning, when communicated along with content containing highly charged emotions.

Emotion bypasses the intellect, reason and understanding. Emotion is a poor vehicle for understanding, thinking and reason are better, and direct observation is the best.

People "think" and deal with the world around them in concepts.

All too often, the majority of their dealings with the world, in all its forms, are a *mental phenomenon* of logically relating mental ideas or concepts with other mental ideas and concepts. But ideas can and often have very little to do with the real world of people and things.

They *could* be more accurately matched to specific existing realities, but more often than not they are not. This is due in part to observational laziness, faulty education, and a lack of an understanding of Man and his mind, but also to intentional deception.

Logic and Concepts

Logic systems demonstrate this well. Math is one example. Set theory is another. You can know and use addition, subtraction, multiplication, division, and algebra, but few of us ever notice that these are complete mental systems of ideas having nothing to do with any actual external reality. How so?

First, the number 1 refers only to a mental concept. One what? How can there be one without having it refer to a specific thing? There is no "one" without a corresponding thing which it refers to anywhere except in our minds.

This is true for all numbers. It's a mental game. This is neither good nor bad. It simply is. But we all think we know what "one" means. We do. But it relates to no specific thing anywhere in all of manifested physical reality. We can *associate* the idea of "one" to "one apple" or "one car" or "one sun", but the concept does not exist anywhere "out there" - it exists completely in our own mind. The notion of "one" unattached to a specific "one thing" simply does not exist anywhere in the entire universe of matter, energy, space and time. But it does exist in our minds.

Second, zero (0) refers to what? A lack of something or anything! It's the complete lack of quantity. Negation! Null and total Void! Some say it refers to the absolute nothingness of deep space. Others describe it as the complete motionlessness of energy. But these are simply more ideas. Where does "zero" exist out in the real world of experience? It doesn't; it's only a mental concept. You can look at an empty place in the sky and say there are "no stars there". But that empty space never had the notion that there were no stars there. The notion doesn't exist "out there". It only exists in a mind. Your mind and my mind!

Third, 1 plus 1 equals 2. Take one orange and place it on the table. Take another one and place it next to the first. Now there are two oranges. Do this for a few other sets of two oranges. The first two oranges don't equal the second or third two sets of oranges. They are different oranges. Again, the concept of addition is a mental notion only. It is useful, yes, but it says nothing about reality, even though we can choose to relate it to reality. Additionally, what does a grain of sand care whether there are 10 grains of sand or 20 grains of sand in close proximity to it? Counting and addition has meaning because conscious, thinking beings give it meaning. It is truly "all in our heads".

Forth, equality doesn't exist anywhere in reality. We say 1 plus 1 "equals" 2. Take two perfectly manufactured German watches and compare them. They look the same, weigh the same, and tell time the same, but they are NOT THE SAME. They are not equal. Even if you could get them completely perfect, which you couldn't, because the atoms and molecules would be different, among other things, in the end they would occupy *different spaces*. You can never make them occupy the same space, try as you might. Equality doesn't exist. But it does in our minds. You can spend the next week trying to find two things "out there" that are truly equal, and you will not be able to. Equality, in reality, doesn't exist anywhere. It never has and it never will. Again, it's a mental notion.

If you believe you have found two things which are truly equal, then you have deluded yourself - your ideas have

94

only given you that notion - but the two things in actuality are not and cannot ever be truly "equal". There are *many* concepts which don't exist and never have existed anywhere, and never will, just as with "equality". But people consider they do just the same. This causes untold trouble when people and groups attempt to force "reality" (i.e. people and society) to conform to their "ideas" about how they imagine people and reality should behave.

Various people and groups promote "social equality" and desire to get all people "equal". This is impossibility and if you notice, it is usually done through some type of force. Chinese and Russian communism systematically murdered millions of people in their attempt to equalize their societies. Again, they tried to eradicate the things which they conceived to act to make people unequal. Get rid of the "rich", the "intelligentsia", and "social inequity".

Socialism taxes heavily the productive and gives to the unproductive in an attempt to "equalize" society - all through force - nobody would pay taxes unless there existed a real potential threat of harm against them. It's all just so much mental dullness, due to taking much too seriously one's own concepts and opinions.

There is nothing wrong with wanting people to be successful and happy, in fact, this is an admirable goal, but forcing them into a controlled "equality" will never do it. Equality does not and cannot exist. It can and does exist *in your mind*, but it will never exist in any external physical universe situation. NEVER!

The best solution for making people happy, successful and productive is to educate them into the nature of their own minds, and apply techniques to expand their mental abilities. No political system or legislation will ever do it. These always deteriorate into examples of enforced mediocrity parading as "fairness", "equality" and "justice".

Fifth, where does division or multiplication occur, as we conceive it, in the external world? It doesn't. It's completely part of a mental logic system which occurs within each of our minds.

The logic systems of math are consistent and work within the framework of the system, but they refer to nothing "out there" really. The point here is that each of us can, and does have, mental ideas about all manner of things, which, while "logically consistent" and seeming to "make sense" within their own framework, have absolutely nothing (or very little) to do with the reality "out there" of mutually shared experience. They follow the rules and laws as *we have defined them*; nothing more and nothing less.

Repeating:

Each of us can, and does have, mental ideas about all manner of things, which, while "logically consistent" and seeming to "make sense" within their own framework, have absolutely nothing (or very little) *to do with the reality "out there" of mutually shared experience. They follow the rules and laws* as we have defined them; *nothing more and nothing less.*

Physical Sciences versus Social Sciences

When we deal with the physical sciences such as chemistry, physics, mechanics, or electronics, we have constructed models of how we conceive these things to

96

operate. These models are useful and have enabled advances of all types in their respective fields. "Science" is "good" in these cases. But again, keep in mind that the model is NOT the thing itself. The physical sciences have been fairly successful, and the concepts and labels have served a useful purpose. It "works" to a large extent. A scientist can tell you *functionally* how electricity works, but what it is *really* is not known.

If a chemist makes a mistake, he learns quickly, because he just blew up his lab and expensive equipment. He adapts his model and changes his theory. If an electronics designer melts a few circuits, in the development of a new microchip, he learns fast, and doesn't make the same mistake again. This works fine as long as it has been applied to the raw physical universe of matter and energy. It hasn't worked fine in the social "sciences". Why?

People are fundamentally "minds". The nature, functioning and potentials of "mind" are radically similar to matter and energy. A mind *interrelates with, uses and controls* matter and energy. This is one of those things you won't necessarily "get" until you experience it for yourself. You can *believe* whatever you like, because that is one of the things minds *always do*, they *believe and become convinced of things*, but your belief won't alter for a second the fact that "mind" is radically similar in some aspects and different in other aspects from the rest of the external physical universe. As an example, where else out there in the physical universe of matter and energy, amidst all space and time, can you find anything which "believes", "considers", "opines" or "attaches significance and meaning". Only sentient beings do that. Minds do that. No rock, brick, bolt of lightning,

97

pulsar, photon, sun, or galaxy ever has or ever will do that. This is a tremendously important distinction which has been lost to most modern fields of study relating to Man and his activities.

There is nothing anywhere which is pure matter or energy which has the capabilities or functions of a conscious mind with the exception of God. In fact, your body doesn't do it either - your mind does it - YOU do it. It would benefit the reader to spend some time considering this. Look around and notice where "beliefs", "ideas" and "meaning" comes from. They come from living conscious beings. Look around more and try to find the formation of a belief or meaning anywhere in the material universe outside of a thinking entity - you won't find it. Keep it to your own personal observation and try to remain honest. "Universal Mind", "Cosmic Consciousness", "Oneness", "Spiritual Unity" and other metaphysical notions have nothing to do with this discussion. The thing I am indicating refers *only* to Man's individual mind, a thing we can all easily observe and become aware of.

Let me see if I can articulate this better. As I stated previously, there is only one element in the universe that is both matter and energy. It is called light. The bible tells us that God is light…listen

But if our gospel be hid, it is hid to them that are lost: In whom the god of this world (Satan) hath blinded the minds of them which believe not, lest the light of the glorious gospel of Christ, who is the image of God, should shine unto them. For we preach not ourselves, but Christ Jesus the Lord; and ourselves your servants for Jesus' sake. For God, who commanded the light to shine out of darkness, hath shined in our

hearts, to *give* the light of the knowledge of the glory of God in the face of Jesus Christ (1Corinthians 4: 3-6).

God is both matter and energy as depicted by Jesus, His Son who came to earth as a man or matter, and the Spirit, which is energy. A person who believes in God has a reality that is controlled by God and operates within a mind that is referred to in the bible as the "Mind of Christ".

"For who hath known the mind of the Lord, that he may instruct him? But we have the mind of Christ" (1 Corinthians 2:16).

A person who doesn't believe in God has a mind that embraces the worldview and his/her reality is controlled by this worldview.

It is meaningless whether "thought" is due to chemical reactions in a brain (which it isn't) or to capabilities all its own. *Functionally*, a mind operates very differently than any observable material thing or phenomena. It does different things entirely.

Psychology and psychiatry, the "modern sciences of the mind", have failed completely to address, delineate, categorize and develop techniques to increase one's awareness of and capabilities of a mind. Psychology, by definition, should be a study of the mind. It isn't anything of the sort within the modern subject. This discussion has much more to do with a valid subject of psychology than either of the modern subjects, which basically ignores the mind.

Of course, an aware being *could* theoretically attach itself to a tree, forest, sun, star or planet, and conceive itself to be this thing, just as we each conceive ourselves to be a

99

human body, and this might prompt a New Ager to proclaim, "See, the sun has feelings", "the Earth has a purpose", or "the universe is sentient". But the situation is no different.

Sentient beings believe themselves to be various things, and experience these things solely due to their total conviction that they are what they conceive themselves to be. The same is true for everything else anyone experiences.

There is no purpose, life or meaning in any aspect of the physical universe, of anything for that matter, other than that given to it be you and me based on our beliefs in God or the worldview. This may sound like humanism or pragmatism (both are worldviews), but what I propose is very far from the views and practical applications of these two approaches to things. Humanism and pragmatism similarly proclaim man and his ideas as the source of everything, but they at the same time tend to still place the physical universe way above the human mind or minds in importance. They place "experience" above all else and concentrate on your "reactions" to it. They tend to greatly diminish your ultimate role in the creation of all your experience. This has drastic practical consequences.

The major impulse of the modern social sciences is to treat Man (and therefore also his mind) as matter and energy. This is not true; a man's body is matter but the mind is not energy. It is the spirit that is energy. The psychologist assumes that what is good for weights, fulcrums and acceleration (i.e. mechanics - a branch of physics) is also good for human beings. Whoops! I am afraid not. Not at all! The psychiatrist assumes that what is good for arthritis and digestive disorders (physical medicine) is also good for "mental disorders". Whoops again. It's just not so! The social planner assumes that what is good for nuclear physics is also good for populations. Once again, whoops! It's not so! And all the college courses, Ph.D.s, psychiatric associations, psychological societies, humanist organizations, behaviorists, geneticists and philosophizing won't make it so. You can believe whatever you choose, but some things remain true regardless of what you believe or how you conceive them to be (this is objective truth!). This is one of those things.

Universes and Reality

The world "out there", external reality, is a mutually shared universe of common experience. It is the lowest common denominator of all our experience. It is the mediocre minimum which we all take for granted and it supplies us with a common field of action. That is all it is.

Your realm of personal "mind" is another sort of universe. You experience it every second of every day. From here comes any and all meaning about anything in the "outer" universe. The functions of attention, concentration, imagination, responsibility, belief, conviction, intention, decision, purpose, reason, intellect, and more solely reside within your own personal "mind". These are qualities of any mind.

The "amount" of each and control we each have over these various functions varies from person to person and even within ourselves from day to day. But they are there in each of us in some form and to some degree. You may

101

be influenced by the external world of common experience, but this inner universe exists, is *very* real, and is ultimately of more value than anything "out there". Why? Because what happens "out there" depends completely on what you do (or what "happens") with your own mind! In fact, your own inner universe is the *only* thing capable anywhere of choosing and deciding value.

The world of external events takes shape in exact accordance with the sum total of all Man's inner beliefs, conviction, ideas, meanings, thoughts, desires, etc.

It is vital to get some grasp of this because Man's inner world, or universe of thought, is very much ignored by all current popular belief systems. This inner universe is *the important universe* and it has been systematically ignored and suppressed by current materialistic notions. The popularization and use of modern psychological and psychiatric theories are the worse example of this. When Man's inner universe is destroyed systematically through institutionalized belief systems, Man can finally become a pale shadow of raw matter and energy, which in itself is dead, meaningless and devoid of all life.

Modern materialism has exaggerated the importance and power of the external universe over the inner universe of Man's mind. Secular Behaviorism talks *ad naseam* about the effect of the environment on people. The environment (external reality) is placed in a superior position above the individual person (mind). People involve themselves in and dissect the physical universe in a futile attempt to gain "understanding".

They think the answers lie outside themselves; that there "good" is somewhere other than where they are. Again, all meaning, purpose and value for anything, is determined by your mind and for you, by your mind alone. You are the most truth you will ever know about anything as you are the ONLY source of truth for everything you experience with the only exception being God and only God! In the end, whatever you end up believing "in" or "about" is fundamentally an *action of your own mind* to attach meaning and significance to something. It's an action of an individual mind but again – God is the only exception!

You are the complete source of meaning for you. You might explain, "I believe this because it's so true, and it makes me feel good, and blah-blah-blah...", and you may attribute your choice to all manner of reasoning about ideas, external events and situations, but in the end

YOU SIMPLY DECIDE TO BELIEVE and EXPERIENCE MEANING solely by your own mental actions.

We all tend to take our cues from external events and our beliefs often follow reactions to events, but this isn't necessary. The function of believing and developing conviction *could* be separate from one's experiences of external reality, and if you suddenly found yourself in some other reality, on some other world, somewhere else, you would simply begin responding to the external events there, and develop new beliefs accordingly. This is as true for science as it is for religion. It is true for everything. Ultimately, nothing is true unless you believe it to be so. And for you, it then is. But *you* are the source of the meaning - the source is not anything you conceive

103

yourself to experience "out there", whether an observable "thing" or an "idea".

The purpose of pointing this out is not to make you feel as if all is useless and meaningless, although this will be the result as long as you look for meaning *outside* yourself and fail to acknowledge your own direct participation in the creation of belief, conviction and meaning for your own personal experience. It's up to you to choose grand beliefs, wondrous convictions, noble purposes and lofty ideals. Then recognizing yourself as the final source of all your meaning, belief and conviction will not degrade into apathy and lack of meaning.

Most people search "out there" to find something to "believe in", and to give their life meaning, but in the end, it is your own action of *establishing belief* which underlies any choice or decision. Again, what you accept to believe need not correspond to any pre-packaged theory, concept or philosophy, whether scientific, philosophical or religious, but we all tend to take for granted that the existing options presented to us are the only possibilities available. But this is difficult to do in a world where Man's inner world and all it does is so casually and persistently denied. It is also difficult to do when so many external forces attempt to sell you on their own specific set of opinions and beliefs. Everybody is trying to get you to accept *their* patterns of belief and systems of meaning.

This is the real battle occurring on planet Earth. The winners and losers of this battle are what truly determine the "evolution" of societies and the world. Now, and in the past, most of what is being sold is

104

trash, as it usually denies and oppresses *that which is capable of believing and attaching meaning* - you and your mind.

Your mind and everyone else's minds are the true source of any quality of life that will ever exist. Solely and completely!

Recognition, education into the functions, and empowerment of minds results in success, decency, morality, strength, sanity and greatness. Denial and suppression of these things results in failure, perversions, immorality, weakness, insanity and mediocrity.

Materialism as a belief system has the effect of denying these things.

Chapter 5 – Reality, Belief and the Mind Section 5

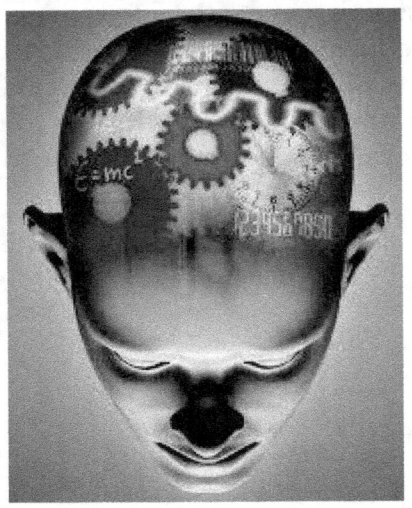

FORCE

The nature of the physical universe is force. Force between matter and force between energy. People don't respond well to force. They never have and they never will. People respond to *understanding, communication* and *learning*. Understanding, communication and learning are functions of minds. There is nothing in the entire physical universe which extends understanding, initiates communication, grants tolerance, promotes compassion or can learn. At least not like a conscious sentient being can understand and learn.

Conscious entities reason, think, initiate action, <u>choose</u> to act morally or immorally, and attach purpose, meaning and "reasons" to everything they see around them and do. No rock, photon, chemical compound, biological organism, or electrical current can or will ever do this. The entirety of the modern social sciences, as they currently exist, directly apply the concepts and approaches derived from an examination of the raw physical universe (modern *physical* science) to Man and minds, with disastrous results (the modern social "sciences" or seeing is believing).

Some may attempt to understand this from the aspect of mind (i.e. behavioral psychology, advertising), but only with an aim at controlling, manipulating, forming and adjusting man's ideas and behaviors for their own purposes. A loftier goal is to educate Man himself into these things, increase his awareness and ability of the functions of his own mind, and let him get on with creating a better world. Treating sentient minds as raw matter is a big error. It is a huge error. War is an example of one group using force to overwhelm another group. A mother smacking her child is another example. Electroshock treatment is another example. Taxation is another example, because if you try to not pay your taxes see what happens - you will be arrested and all your possessions will be forcibly taken from you. Burning heretics at the stake or torturing them is another example. What these all have in common is *the application of force, or the threat of force, to minds in an attempt to exact compliance to someone's notions of what you should do, think or say.*

Force!

It's not good for living things. It suppresses and denies self-determinism, creativity and responsibility. That's partially why socialism and communism can never "work". Capitalism also can never work though, because while presented as a "free competitive system", it is actually not this at all - it's a very small group of extremely wealthy people controlling everything and ensuring they remain in control. Their goal is *total* control and they use every aspect of modern culture to achieve this aim. This is the true meaning of the term "new world order".

The modern "science" of behaviorism has its source in the same flawed notions. People are treated like rocks, bricks and "stuff". If you push on a rock a certain way it will move a certain way. If you heat up a chemical a certain way it will melt or change to a gas in a certain exact way. If you send a current through certain electrical components a certain way, certain exact repeatable results are obtained. The crazy secular behavioral "scientists" think that if you apply the right force to people in a certain way, then they will "behave" a certain way. And this is true sadly enough because when minds are treated as matter or energy, in the same way utilizing force against them, the power, ability and potential of their minds is reduced and the mind begins to *mimic* matter and energy. This is not a good thing and it is true only in a degraded and "lower" manner. How?

A healthy, unoppressed human being tends to create and cause the environment to align with his wishes or

108

intentions. **He makes things, builds things, and puts things there which weren't there before (whether it be an opera, book, garden, house, painting, marriage, business, friendship, relationship, club, or whatever). A mind in good shape, and left free of force, creates using whatever is available (vision). But when force is applied to a mind, it deteriorates and begins mimicking matter. What is the nature of matter? It is non-sentient, non-causative and tends to follow strict laws and rules. It responds - it doesn't initiate. It obeys unquestioningly. If an object is set in motion it tends to stay in motion unless stopped by an opposing force (such as friction or a barrier). Electricity flows when the battery is connected to the circuit and it stops flowing when the battery connection is broken. <u>Matter creates nothing. It builds nothing. It starts nothing. It understands nothing at all</u>. It's all about energy – SPIRIT!**

When Man and his mind are treated in the same way as matter, he falls away from his nature as a creative agent and becomes like a rock - he gets pushed, shoved, forced, ordered, and basically stops doing what he should be doing - creating the world around him. Ideally, this is done responsibly, joyfully, intelligently and sanely. This is quite impossible when Man is treated as matter, "stuff, or an "animal" (stimulus-response methods).

Man's "mind" is a different thing and of a different nature entirely. Modern "materialism" has discarded any notion of Man's mind. It is irrelevant to this discussion whether man's mind is part of his "soul" or "spirit". I am not talking "religion", "spiritualism" or anything else. *Functionally*, whatever its actual source, Man's mind exists, is observable to each of us, and possesses qualities

109

and capabilities found nowhere else in the entire physical universe.

The secular behavioral scientist, psychologist, psychiatrist, and social planner say they are trying to discover the "laws" of man and societies. So they experiment upon people with drugs, electricity, surgery and social control. The *true* laws are partially explained here. Man is mind above all else. Man's *mind* creates the world in all its aspects. There are no *natural* laws of people and societies except as explained by Man's mind, its capabilities, and what it does.

Various study within the subject of sociology which examine Man's societies and activities of the past are a complete waste of time if the view is to "figure out Man" and what he is. Man can only be understood by understanding Man's mind. What it is and what it does. This is not "religious", "philosophical" or "opinion". Just look at what minds do, especially your own mind, as that is the only mind you really can know.

Minds place attention, desire, intend, create, imagine, think, believe, consider, plan, envision, choose, observe, bestow meaning, agree on purposes, and initiate action. There is more to it, but the basic idea is explained here, and it is radically different from what the modern proponents of materialism propose and enforce on modern man. All they do is enforce upon Man the image of him as an animal, as matter and energy. Their approach is to *control* him. They have neglected the mind completely, with very negative results. They have removed the "being" from a "human being" and simply have left the animal part - the "human".

110

Man is NOT only a biological organism. In fact, this is actually the "smaller" part of what he is. His true nature resides in what we conceive to be "mind". This is where all his power, ability and greatness reside. It is grossly neglected, ignored and largely forgotten. And it has been suppressed by most religions as well as social institutions throughout history.

Buddhism and the Vedic literature of the Hindus *have* examined Man as mind, and while having practical methods to realize and expand some of these things, they have also largely failed to disseminate it in a way acceptable and useful to Mankind. Much of Eastern religion and philosophy is fundamentally *psychology*, and not religion. Western thought has misunderstood the actual meanings, partially due to their own tendency to "intellectualize," but also because the subjects themselves are mired in opinions, Eastern cultural notions, and arbitrary religious connotations. This is the position modern psychology, psychiatry and social planning has placed modern Man. His mind has been forgotten in favor of genetics, behaviorism and biochemistry. They all depend on force, to some degree and in some form, to get their results. Crime and violence is not rising because of TV. It's rising because Man is viewed as just so many bricks.

Morality isn't deteriorating because of a lack of religion, it's because the social planners completely believe Man only needs to be placed into suitable controlled environments to "bring out" the ideal "social Man" (as they conceive this to be). Modern "mental health" isn't failing because of chemical brain imbalances or "bad genes", but because psychiatry applies *force* to minds - physically in the form of involuntary commitment,

111

restraints, strait jackets, and lobotomies, electrically in the form of electric shock treatments, and chemically in the form of drugs.

Social, national and international unrest continue unabated because instead of appealing to understanding, communication, and granting understanding to others (all mind functions), every nation and group in the world uses physical force or deceit (using the mind capabilities incorrectly and dishonestly) to get their messages across and to realize their goals. There is no social, economic or political "system" which can or will make for a decent world utilizing force - and they ALL depend on force. Only the recognition and nurturing of Man and his inherent qualities of "mind" can do this.

When Man's mind is neglected and discarded as unimportant, so disappears decency, responsibility, creativity and respect. Every time someone of some group tries to make you believe what they believe, your right as a choosing being is denied, because your true capabilities as a conscious entity, able to choose belief and determine meaning for yourself, is ignored. This is violated by most people and groups today, due to a lack of understanding of what Man, as a mind, actually is, and conceiving Man to be something else.

It is impossible to "respect" a rock, a molecule or lightning bolt. You might *appreciate* or *admire* its organization and subtle arrangement, but notice again, that it is *your mind* alone which has the capability to admire and appreciate. The qualities of admiration and appreciation (amongst many others) are not inherent in physical things although they can be *bestowed upon*, *identified with* or *attached to* physical things by the

112

action of conscious minds. The reason I stated in the beginning that most educated people are "not smart" is because the social sciences are studied, accepted, believed and followed without a second thought.

Yes, many of these college students, and Ph.D.s probably got A's, can discuss all manner of complex topics, and are viewed as "smart" by their fellows. Within their respective subjects and systems of thought, they can remain logically consistent and appear to be "right". But, they have failed completely to ever honestly compare the reality of people and their own minds with the destructive results of their arbitrary theories and beliefs. Why? Because they learned ideas and concepts, got real good at playing with these ideas and concepts, but never once imagined that their systems of thought were fundamentally flawed. It's ironic.

Man's modern mind has conceived systems of thought (materialism, modern psychology, psychiatry), which act to deny the very existence of that which did the conceiving! Man believes things which deny his tendency to create belief. Man is convinced of things which ignore his ability to establish conviction. Man has opinions which act to invalidate the value of his opinions.

Materialism - its True Failure

As systems of logic, the social sciences are fine. The notions, ideas, postulates and theories all make sense *within their own framework*, but the big problem is that the most basic axioms are false. Man is NOT matter or energy at his most basic level - at least he doesn't *function* that way when he is in good shape. As anyone knows who has studied logic systems, any system falls apart once the basic axioms are found to be flawed. As I said earlier, if a chemist makes a mistake and blows up his lab, he can adjust his theory, remake his understanding of the laws or rules involved, and not make the same error again. He learns fast, out of necessity.

The same is not true when dealing with people and societies. It takes years and even decades or centuries to realize mistakes have been made. And many people are abused, hurt, and killed along the way. Look at Communism - Karl Marx, Lenin and Stalin believed the ideology of Communism to be "scientific" and based upon "modern scientific social observations". Seventy years and millions of butchered people proved the notion flawed. But what was the cost? We don't have the luxury of treating all humanity and his civilizations as giant labs to run social, religious and political experiments in. Plus, in case you haven't noticed, those who believe all the current social and psychological theories are completely unwilling to entertain even the remotest possibility that their ideas are flawed.

Materialism, when applied to human beings, *always* has devastating results. Look around. It's vividly apparent wherever one looks. There will never be a "good" result where materialism is applied to sentient, conscious beings. There will be greater enforced control, less freedom, and humanity will fade and eventually die out as a species, because the most fundamental aspect of Man, his mind, is denied theoretically and practically through modern flawed "scientific" belief systems. This is equally true for past and present religions, just as it is for modern "science", wherever force, or threats of force, are used to exact adherence to opinions and beliefs.

114

This is not an argument of materialism versus spirituality. Almost all historical periods, even when characterized by "religious" or "spiritual" influences, have been actually "materialistic" because Man's mind was largely neglected and oppressed in favor of arbitrary belief systems about the physical universe and man's relationship to it. The history of this planet has been mainly characterized by the use of force against Man and his mind to alter belief and behavior, whether these forces were "religious", "political", "economic" or "social". Any perceived dichotomy of "materialism" versus "spirituality" is an illusion and is not part of this discussion. Materialism here means the viewing of everything as inherently physical, with the neglect of man's mind a usual by-product of such a view. Religions have done this as much as any modern "scientific" materialism.

Actually, calling educated people "dumb" is incorrect. Intelligence or "being smart" is primarily characterized by one's ability to understand concepts, relate them to other concepts, and use them together within a complete unique system or field. But as was shown with logic and math, being good at and understanding the axioms, suppositions and concepts of any specific system in no way necessitates any exact or real correlation to anything in the real world of observable facts and situations. This has never been truer than in the case of modern psychology, psychiatry and social planning (people control). It's not that these people aren't "smart". They are often very smart - they have simply been taught and believe false ideas. It's their personal observation and moral integrity which have failed. Also, intelligence has nothing to do with compassion, understanding or decency. There have been *brilliant brutes* and *uneducated*

115

humanitarians. Psychiatrists tend to fall within the first group.

The modern educated member of any of the social "sciences", while possibly very "smart", has completely missed the boat, believed completely what has been taught to them, failed to ever view the actual results of their practices, and have propagated severely destructive theories and applications in modern societies. What has made it so much worse is that governments and major financial interests all over the world have funded, agreed with, and supported modern psychology, psychiatry and social control. Why? The answer to that is easy. They think they know what's best for you and they will do whatever they have to do to bring about their notion of an "ordered and well controlled world". They would like you all to act like matter - like bricks - to obey faithfully every order given you, without thought or personal decision. Their notion of an ideal world seems to be one characterized by "order", "predictability" and "harmony". These are actually characteristics of *matter*, and have no place in a sane and creative world of responsible and competent people. Making sane, creative, and competent people *should* be the goal of any "mental health system", and making a safe society where honest people can function at their best should be the goal of a proper government. Neither exists today.

Sadly, no existing popular or official field of study or subject so much as even desires such a thing. Current Earth is in a sad state of affairs. This is a direct result of applying ideas about the physical world and physical sciences directly to Man, his mind, and his societies.

The current governments and major world financial concerns view Man as just so many bricks to be manipulated controlled and forced into proper action or subservience. Much of their actions are most likely due to complete ignorance to the truth of what is stated in this essay. But I suspect there are some who know the truth of what I am discussing here, and they choose to do it anyway. You will not find a more blatant example of pure evil anywhere. One of the worst things you can do to any person or society is force them or it to become like matter and energy, because when this is done every vestige of humanity and what makes Man decent and great disappears. He becomes a rock, waiting to be acted upon by an outside force, never initiating anything original, creative or decent. Actually, it's worse than that. He becomes a combination of the worse Man can be. Welcome to the 21st century.

Every horror done by and on human beings throughout the entire known (and unknown) history of this planet can be explained by Man having been treated as matter and failing to extend to, grant, and nurture within him understanding, ability, communication, awareness, and personal power as a creative thinking being - a mind.

This may sound strangely "mystical" or "religious" to some. It is neither, and is only raw simple truth. Those who would deny Man's right as a free mind, with creativity, awareness and responsibility are consigning him to oblivion. Regardless of the excuses, justifications or concatenations of logic used by the atheist, materialist, humanist, militarist, nationalist, politician, psychiatrist or religionist, the results are always the same - pain, misery, failure and death.

117

Whenever man's true mind and awareness, and all its powers and functions are denied, there goes the entire civilization. Force reigns. It has happened before, and it is happening now. This has been the pattern throughout all human history.

There has never been a time where an educated society was taught about their own mind, what it is, how it operates, and with the intention to increase their personal awareness, understanding, ability, power, creativity and success. In fact, Man and his mind have never been adequately studied within any "official" subject, with an aim at doing this. It need not be that way.

Responsibility is a function of a creative mind that is allowed and encouraged to be a creative mind. So are decency, honesty and morality. In a world which suppresses man and his mind, these things disappear - and so they are disappearing in modern civilizations. This is the true source of the world's trouble. It is nothing else. Every other thing or influence which has been cited as a cause, whether political, social, economic, racial, or religious, has this as its true fundamental explanation. These other situations couldn't exist if the basic ideas in this essay weren't ignored, violated and suppressed. Psychiatric methods inhibit and harm minds, and thereby also harm everything a mind can and should do. Behavioral psychology methods force compliance. Social control manipulates and deceives through mis-education and outright dissemination of lies.

There is only one way to bring about a better world where people can be happy, successful, and free of crime, war, insanity and poverty. As said before, the solution resides in no "system". The solution lies in recognizing, encouraging, and bringing about increased personal ability in each and every human being - through the recognition and nurturing of "mind" functions. And then *let them all, as a unit, create whatever world they so desire*. But this is so very far from the view of any current established theory, belief or practice on this planet at this time. This view, if practiced would destroy almost every extant social, political, and religious institution (remember, religion is man-made). There are too many people who have much to lose (from their viewpoint and set of beliefs) by the enactment of such a situation. Empowering people threatens them all.

The world at any time is only the sum totals of what people conceive it to be. When they have unclear understandings, vague notions, incorrect conceptions, and false beliefs about themselves and others, the world follows accordingly. Until a majority of the individual people, as creative minds, obtain an accurate understanding of the nature, functions, and capabilities of their own minds, and actually *use* effective methods to improve the operation of their own minds, the world will continue as it has always and as it is now - chaotic, uncontrollable, violent, oppressive, and failing. The only reason various segments of societies and the world still appear sane, decent and productive is because Man's mind is strong and resilient, and often manifests its inherent natural tendencies *despite* the continual efforts against it not to do so. But this will become less and less as more freedom is denied, and as popular psychological and psychiatric theories are increasingly applied to the world's populations.

Chapter 6 – Reality, Belief and the Mind Section 6

Examples

Religion

Most religions are control mechanisms and this applies to all the "big ones" and not only to modern "cults". Religion is man-made and not God-made. The people are fed largely untrue notions about deity, the universe and his relationship to these, and they are forced to accept, adhere to and promote these ideas under the threat of duress or worse. Much religion to this day is still characterized by arguments, fighting and outright warring. It is often a matter or "power" - power over the lives, thoughts and actions of others. One group "believes" their notions implicitly and demands everyone else accepts them or else. Various "reasoning", "spiritual posturing", excuses and justifications are used. Again, it all makes sense within each unique religious belief system. You see an example of this almost every day in the media. Remember, ideas and concepts are largely in Man's mind alone. This is no less true for religious ideas. The fanatical religious person may *claim* his basic axioms and assumptions are true, but he should have no right to enforce them on anybody in any way. It is up to you to decide just how much of some religious idea has anything to do with any objective reality or fact. You should be granted the right to freely decide and choose. You rarely are. It's not that "religion" is bad. We would, for the most part, feel a large emptiness without it. It is the "use" of religion which has too often been badly practiced. These are two different things.

DO NOT CONFUSE RELIGION WITH GOD! Believers in God follow only God; they follow no man and no worldview. Christians go to church but a church is not the building; it is the congregants that make up the church – the body of Christ. The Christian faith has hundreds of denominations due to various interpretations of God's Word; however a true church is one that believes and follows the essential doctrines of the historic Christian faith. Christianity is a lifestyle built on a relationship with God. It is not open to interpretation, and in fact it states in the New Testament that it is the Spirit's job to interpret the Word of God.

121

Psychiatry & Materialism

"Science", modern psychology and psychiatry function as modern "religions" in that they are firmly believed and enforced on everyone else whether you agree with them or not. As psychiatry obtains greater and greater government support, this becomes even truer.

Psychiatric views have infiltrated the legal, various social, governmental and educational systems. It is heavily funded and your tax dollars support it (whether you like it or not).

Psychiatry also possesses the tools of enforcement and social control which modern governments adore. But, ultimately it is only *just another belief system*, quite arbitrary and *very false*, once again allied with governments (the State) and used to oppress the public.

Strangely the humanist will understand this idea completely about traditional religions throughout history, but fail completely to see how this applies to psychiatry and its pretended association with modern science.

Religions have a historical tendency to align with sectarian powers (i.e. governments - the State). Whenever this has been done, the State has often promoted one religion above all others, and tended to suppress differing religious views. This is why the First Amendment to the Constitution was written:

Congress shall make no law respecting the establishment of religion, or prohibiting the free exercise thereof; or abridging the freedom of speech, or of the press; or the right of the people peaceably to assemble and to petition the Government for a redress of grievances.

This was designed to prevent the State from supporting one religious view over others. The government *should* be separate from any religion (separation of Church and State), but it should also be kept separate from ANY belief system - materialism, psychiatry, behaviorism, eugenics, genetics, biopharmacology, and biochemistry included! No government funds should go to *any* belief system, religious *or scientific*.

"Religion" and "science" differ only in name - ultimately they are each only unique *belief systems*. They exist in different places on the "belief spectrum". Enforcing either one on the public has negative results. Personally, I don't want my children forced to study and believe the theory of evolution, which is incorrect as far as I am concerned. It's not a matter of evolution against creationism. It's not religion against science. One needs to rise above the false ideas and apparent dichotomies, and learn to see from a "higher ground". You should have the right to believe whatever *you choose* to believe but *nothing* should be mandatory. Public schools, supported by the government, promote the materialistic approach. They shouldn't, just as they shouldn't promote any specific religious approach.

Ayn Rand said it well in discussing the traditional battle between the extremes of rationalism and empiricism (spiritualism vs. materialism; religion vs. science):

In the title essay of For the New Intellectual, discussing modem philosophy's concerted attack on man's mind, I referred to the philosophers' division into two camps, "those who claimed that man obtains his knowledge of the world by deducing it exclusively from concepts, which come from inside his head and are not derived from the perception of physical facts (the Rationalists) -and those who claimed that man obtains his knowledge from experience, which was held to mean: by direct perception of immediate facts, with no recourse to concepts (the Empiricists). To put it more simply: those who joined the Witch Doctor, by abandoning reality - and those who clung to reality, by abandoning their mind.

This has been the established defined boundaries of the "battle" within traditional philosophy and western culture. It is a barren playing field as it gives complete loss and failure whichever side one chooses. It's either "all-mind" in a mystical muddle of conceptual absurdities, or it is "all-physical matter" in a materialistic mindlessness of biological superiority and temporal hedonism. And in the end both resort to force to secure acceptance and adherence.

The modern behavioral psychologist and psychiatrist are avid proponents of the second school - empiricists - they have totally abandoned the mind. A "science" of Man can never achieve or excel when it denies the very thing which creates any "science" - Man's mind. Modern psychology, which by definition is "the study of the mind", ignores and denies the very object of its own subject!

Materialism, the "scientific approach", humanism, realism, pragmatism, or whatever you want to call it are simply *ideologies*, containing a unique combination of ideas and beliefs, and more often than not, orthodoxies - demanding that one conform to certain traditional or currently accepted beliefs and ideas.

Materialism, just as any religion, is a unique set of axioms, assumptions, opinions and beliefs about the

124

nature of Man, the universe, and how Man relates to the universe. It is a system of <u>concepts</u> about reality, and nothing more.

The constitutional amendment written to separate Church and State should have been written to keep ALL belief systems away from government acceptance, subsidization and support. Currently the governments of the United States and Europe are so tied up with these other interests that it may be impossible to separate them.

The intent of this amendment was to allow people, *through their own conscience*, to decide what to believe and support. I don't want to pay taxes which fund studies or organizations which drug children with Ritalin, encourage electric shock of the elderly, or act to degrade Man's view of himself into that of an animal. But I *am* forced to support the modern religion of materialism. I hope some bright constitutional scholar and lawyer will someday, soon, take this to the courts and straighten this out.

"Modern" educated people think they have risen above "the absurd and childish beliefs of past religions", but, in fact, they have not risen anywhere. They have simply *switched* to another, equally absurd and flawed, set of beliefs. Of course, they don't, and cannot see this, much less understand it, because *they are believers too* - just as were the religious folks in past centuries.

The materialist or psychiatrist is equally convinced of his possession of the "truth", just as was any well-educated priest of the Spanish Inquisition (and the Priests were often *very highly* educated, in fact, more than anyone else). There is no difference in how either functions; they each have a unique package of opinions, beliefs, and convictions about Man and the universe, they each believe they are "right", and they are willing to happily force everyone else to believe the same things as they do. They are both totalitarians. They are both the victims of their own over-active conceptualizing, which they each take much too seriously and attribute far too much importance to.

Psychiatry and modern psychology, functioning as materialistic interpretations of Man and life, act as a unique set of opinions and beliefs about man and the universe, just as any religious or philosophical system.

Each is a unique set of axioms, assumptions, opinions and beliefs about the nature of Man and the universe. They are logical and well-organized structures of *concepts* and *ideas* only, but factually, very far removed from any actual correspondence to existing realities.

If you honestly read through these pages, and follow up with some of the reference books, you will come to understand how this is so. But if you don't, you will stay fixedly set in your own very limited conceptual framework of reality. What most of us think about reality is not *what is*, but only what we conceive it to be! The two are, more often than not, worlds apart.

Religions, in the past, allied with governmental powers to forward their beliefs, through force and oppression. This is what the first constitutional amendment was designed to prevent for reoccurring. *This* is what should be separated from the State:

-- ANY set of beliefs regarding Man, the universe and his relationship to it. "Materialism", "psychology" and "psychiatry" are exactly this. The "religion" of

materialism is very much connected to the State, and promoted by the State. It shouldn't be. It functions as a "religion" in exactly the same way as anything usually called a "religion".

A "religion" is only a unique sub-category of a larger category - any ideology or philosophy concerning Man, the universe and Man's relationship to the universe. The amendment should have read, or should be changed to read:

Congress shall make no law respecting the establishment of any ideology or belief system, or prohibiting the free exercise thereof; or abridging the freedom of speech, or of the press; or the right of the people peaceably to assemble and to petition the Government for a redress of grievances.

The religious proponents in the past believed their ideas completely and justified their oppressive actions because it was "truth" (to them). The proponents of "materialism", psychiatry, psychology and modern "science" *believe* completely, and in exactly the same way, that their ideas are "modern" and "correct", and also similarly justify their destructive actions because it is the "truth" (to them). Neither ever thought they were doing anything wrong, and in fact, both believe they are doing the most wonderful of things! This was and is complete delusion. It was true then, in the past, with religious persecution, and it is true now with modern behavioral psychology and psychiatry.

There is *no* difference between the two; none at all. This is often difficult for "modern people" to see, because one tends to become "stuck" within their own strictly defined belief system (which they don't recognize as a belief

127

system but instead, see as their own perception of "truth"), but it is completely true nonetheless.

Sadly, the Constitutional fathers of this country didn't perceive the first amendment in this larger framework, and the amendment wasn't written in this broader context, otherwise the current abuses could have been prevented.

It is sad that every period of history, including our own, is characterized by people who consider themselves supremely intelligent, in-the-know, aware of "the truth", smarter, and who are completely willing to enforce their beliefs and opinions upon everybody else (whether in the name of "religion" or "science"). The modern materialist, in the form of the psychiatrists and psychologists, are doing this more than it has ever been done before - in both quantity and quality of abuse. Hopefully the realization and application of this doesn't come too late.

Government

Most governments are controlled by people who think they know what is best for everyone else, or who use governments to implement their own personal social, financial, or religious ideas on the general public and on other countries. Again, examples appear daily in the media, although usually never delineated clearly as to true causes.

The US Government was used by large commercial interests to fight the Gulf War. This is only one example of many where governments are actually pawns of the true powers which use them for their own ends.

Almost every president, cabinet member, and government leader is controlled by (supported and bought) or an existing member of large financial or corporate interests.

128

Where do you think their true allegiance lies? Usually, most government people go back to work for or begin to work for the corporate entities they have been supporting all along while part of any government.

The FDA (food and drug administration), a government agency, monitors, approves, and controls "drugs" and supposedly is concerned for the safety of the public. Many members of the FDA Board are past executives of major drug companies, and often go to work as executives (with big salaries) in major drug companies when completing their stint in the FDA (as a reward). Is it any wonder drugs continue to be promoted despite obvious dangers and harms, and alternative, yet often safer, practices continually undergo severe attacks and suppression?

The FDA is a promotional and enforcement arm of the major drug companies, and NOT an honest public service group of objective citizens. This tendency is true throughout all aspects of modern governments, although very much hidden from the public's perception.

Communication versus Force

Here's another slant on the whole thing. Each person and group anywhere basically has their own unique views and ideas and wants to get these accepted by others. This can be anything from a personal like for a music group, to ones infatuation with an artist, to religion, to politics. Why? I don't know. They just do; its part of the nature of sentient beings.

A being's idea or belief, when accepted by others, obtains more agreement and thereby becomes more "real". It's just his way of creating something, putting it "out there", and giving it more "staying power" - it lasts longer when more people agree with it.

So everyone is trying to get everyone else to agree with them and to contribute to their ideas, whatever they may be.

There's nothing wrong with that. That's the nature of life. Ideally, sane, decent and capable beings would *communicate* with others with an intention to bring about an understanding and agreement with what they believe in the other person. It would all be very "above boards", voluntary, and freely accepted or not. No one would get mad if you didn't accept and contribute to the idea.

But apparently that is much too difficult for most people and groups on this planet, because instead, what is largely used is force, in the form of guns, threats, condescension, ridicule, controlled mass media, social control, brain washing, slanted indoctrination, covert intelligence operations, military action, deceit, sly persuasion, electric shock, drugs, lobotomies, brain microchip implants and all forms of manipulation.

People and groups fail with communication and then resort to force, deceit and trickery. These exist in various forms to some degree in personal lives, business, relationships, government, religion, and all aspects of society. Volumes of books could be written on specific examples. Any patient and honest observer can find many examples of each. It has been the *modus operandi* for most of Earth's history.

It would benefit anyone to sit down and spend a few hours examining this. Start with the area of personal life, and locate a few examples where someone has failed at getting another to think or do (behave) as they desired, and then resorted to force or deceit in some form to attempt to realize their wishes. Many male-female relationships provide ample substance for this. Do the same for the areas of business, government, and religion.

Force is applied to get others to think, behave and believe as others want them to. This tendency continues unabated. It has been with us all throughout human history and it is with us now. In fact, with modern mass media, technology, drugs, behavioral techniques, and thought manipulation it is continuing at an ever expanding rate. If you don't see it, or don't see the magnitude of it, it simply means they have done their jobs well, because part of the modern methods includes the desire to remain hidden and anonymous. But it is happening just the same.

While most everything is "only ideas and concepts", there *are* ideas and concepts which more closely align with actual events and situations. All concepts are not equal as to their accurate relationship to the things, events and relationships they refer to. What has just been described is not an illusion like most people's understanding of "gravity".

The ideas discussed here have a close association with actual situations and events. The mind of man exists as described here. The current cultural problems exist. Materialism is the primary culprit. These exist no matter what your opinion or concept about them may be.

You can choose to *believe* that

1) Man's mind doesn't exist

2) Consciousness and human activity is biochemical or stimulus-response in nature

3) Is meaningless as a factor in anything, but all you will be doing is *exercising a function of the very mind you deny to exist* - the capability and tendency to create belief.

There are real situations occurring on the planet now. Take the time to find out for yourself what these are. They are not what you have been led to believe.

The Definition of "Psychology"

The word "psychology" is the combination of two terms - study (ology) and soul (psyche), or mind. The derivation of the word from Latin gives it this clear and obvious meaning:

The study of the soul or mind!

This meaning has been altered over the years until today this is not what the word means at all. The subject of psychology, as studied in colleges and universities, currently has very little to do with the mind, and absolutely nothing to do with the soul or spirit.

It is important to understand that words and ideas are supposed to refer to something. "The large tree in the front yard" refers to an actual thing that can be seen, touched and experienced. "The man walking his little dog last night at sunset" refers to an actual event that can be seen, observed and experienced. The realm of mind is an actual realm that can be experienced, and at one time there were words that accurately referred to this realm.

Let's see what a few dictionaries have to say and how a word could alter and lose its true and actual meaning.

132

"Psyche" is defined as:

1. The spirit or soul.
2. The human mind.
3. In psychoanalysis, the mind functioning as the center of thought, emotion, and behavior.

And defining "soul", we have:

1. The physical manifestations of the body combined with the immortal elements in a person.
2. A person's mental or moral or emotional nature.

Most of us would agree we have a "psyche" per the above definitions in the sense of mind, thought, and emotions. Most would also agree they have a "soul" per the second definition above relating to man's mental, moral or emotional nature. We might all have different notions about what these ultimately are, but few could sanely disagree they exist.

The derivation of "psyche" comes from Latin and the Greek *psukhe* - breath, life, soul. To get a better "feel" for this term try to think of it as the invisible animating principle or entity that occupies, interacts with and directs the physical body.

We are not dealing with opinions or beliefs here. This is simply what the words and terms mean. Get clear on this first and understand what the words and terms mean, before you start getting into the opinions of others on the subject. If you choose to decide the "mind" refers to nothing real after understanding what the words and definitions mean, despite the fact that almost 6,000 years of thinking men have seriously and carefully looked into this subject, and after no real investigation on your own part, then that's your decision.

Also, realize you will be basing this decision on "thinking" and "reason", both of which are only subsidiary to and *part* of any one mind, and neglecting to use a greater aspect of your mind - your personal awareness and direct observation.

Basing a decision on what other people say about a mind involves only *concepts* and *ideas* about a mind. Observation involves *experiencing the mind itself* - your own mind. When it comes to minds there is only one mind any of us can directly observe or experience and that mind is our own.

If you want to learn about minds, the only place to start is with your own. You cannot directly observe or experience the mind of another person, at least not without some extrasensory ability such as telepathy.

What is the Mind?

Originally, and for thousands of years, the subject of psychology involved the study of the human spirit, soul or mind. This involves things and functions not obviously visible to the physical senses. You can't see a mind with one's eyes. You can't "feel" a thought with one's hands. You can't place an emotion on a scale and weigh it. You can't detect imagination, even with sophisticated electronic detection devices. Just because some scientist's electronic device measures various electronic pulses or signals when you are asked to imagine something does not at all mean that they are "measuring imagination". What they are measuring is some brain reaction that occurs *when* you initiate an act of imagination. There *is* a relationship between the mind and the brain, but this relationship is almost completely unknown and not

134

understood. The same is true for any chemical reactions or events that occur concurrent with imagination, thoughts or feelings. There *is* some relationship, but it is poorly understood. In fact, the entire framework of the relationship is poorly conceived. Modern "scientific" fields, since they haven't been able to study or detect these things with the physical senses or laboratory measuring devices have taken a drastic leap and declared that these things therefore don't exist. They have therefore asserted that these things don't deserve recognition, and should be ignored in any "legitimate" study of man, the mind, and human behavior. John Watson, a typical secular behavioral psychologist had this to say:

The extent to which most of us are shot through with a savage background is almost unbelievable.... One example of such a religious concept is that every individual has a soul *which is separate and distinct from the body.... No one has ever touched a soul, or seen one in a test tube, or has in any way come into relationship with it as he has with the other objects of his daily experience...*

The secular behaviorist asks: Why don't we make what we can observe *the real field of psychology? Let us limit ourselves to things that can be observed, and formulate laws concerning only those things. Now what can we observe? We can observe* behavior - *what the organism does or says. And let us point out at once: that* saying *is doing - that is,* behaving . . . . - John Watson, behaviorist

Strangely, the study of the mind has come into the peculiar position of being a study that denies the mind! That's like biology denying the existence of

135

biological organisms, but going on pretending to still be the science of biological organisms while actually dealing with something else entirely. A subject can't exist if it denies the very basis of its own existence by definition. That is the state of modern western psychology and psychiatry. Mmmm? They can't and shouldn't exist, but they do. The entire structure of these subjects as they currently exist is a sham.

Let's take a closer look at this. We each are quite aware we have a mind, emotions, and thoughts, even if we are not so clear or sure about the "soul" and "spirit".

We know we are aware and possess self-awareness, but what the nature, qualities and potentials are of awareness is largely anybody's guess.

We each know we possess consciousness. In fact, we are aware of our own consciousness as much or more than anything else, yet modern "science" ignores and even denies it. But the truth, despite what "science" or "professionals" say, is that the mind exists to and for each of us as an obvious and observable fact of direct experience. A quick look can tell us many obvious things.

I doubt any of us would suggest we don't have a mind, awareness, thoughts or feelings even though none of these things can be detected or perceived with the physical senses or "scientific" measuring gadgets. No third party observer can directly observe or detect *any* of these things. *We don't immediately run off and deny their existence* and we correctly assume others have similar minds, thoughts, feelings and emotions. They do. Modern psychologists and psychiatrists, for all practical purposes, completely deny every aspect of the invisible world known to you as your mind. It *is* invisible to physical detection, but it *does* exist. In fact, it very much exists, but it is not made up of anything physical. While the mind deals with and relates to some subtle forms of energy, in the end it cannot be understood within the framework of matter or energy. Of course, any card-carrying materialist naturally hates that idea with a passion. To them, "if I can't measure it then it doesn't exist".

There is constant activity within each of our "invisible worlds". We are each in some way constantly analyzing problems, entertaining thoughts of tomorrow's occurrences, recalling yesterday's failures, wallowing in the sadness of a loss, concentrating on the creation of a musical composition, or day-dreaming. There are ever changing feelings and emotions about everything we experience, and an endless parade of judgments and commentary about what we see. Actually, for many of us, we have *too much* mind. It goes on and on and never seems to stop. It is a constant source of images, memories and ideas intruding themselves upon our awareness. Most of us can't control any of this and simply accept as inevitable this continual parade of images and ideas appearing across the landscape of our mind.

In a very real manner *all problems* with any mind, such as things psychiatry calls "depression", "anxiety", "compulsive disorder", "Attention Deficit Disorder" (ADD or ADHD), and even "suicidal ideation", are ultimately and solely *uncontrollable aspects of one's own mind that intrude upon the person's awareness*. It's not that these things don't exist in some way, but they don't exist in the way psychiatry understands and claims to solve them. A better way to handle these problems would be to assist

137

the person to *increase control over the content of their own mind*. There are many ways to do this, although they have never been all pulled together, adequately investigated, codified and organized into a straight-forward workable compilation of methods. Modern "science" has simply discarded the notion of the mind, and from that point on, never bothered to investigate it closely with the aim to understand, solve or improve it.

First, this invisible world *is* totally real. It is *not* imaginary or a hallucination. My invisible world isn't directly real to you, and your invisible world isn't directly real to me, but they are *each real nonetheless*. The person who wants to argue this fact is simply a fool, dull, unable to comfortably observe his *own* mind (because it is possibly filled with degraded and nasty things), and probably addicted to the objects of physical sensation and perception to the exclusion of anything else (a modern materialist).

Second, this "invisible" world of mind involves many different aspects, functions and potentials. Imaginations, attention, intellect, awareness, intention, reason, will, responsibility, memory, and many other things exist in each of us. They are a vital and important part of us. Some people might venture to say some of these things ARE us. There is much to each of these areas and a short attempt to articulate them cannot begin to even scratch the surface of their nature, functioning, possible development and capabilities. But they definitely *do exist* and deserve recognition and attention. Any subject calling itself "psychology" would have to address *these things* in detail. The failure of modern psychology and psychiatry to do so is glaringly apparent. These subjects now only address behavior, physiology, genetics and biochemistry, and the mind is of no real concern. *That* is a very sad comment on the current state of "modern psychology".

Psychology Definition Altered

Let's return now to the dictionary definitions of "psychology".

From the *Oxford American Dictionary*:

1. The study of the mind and how it works.
2. Mental characteristics, *can you understand his psychology?*

That's fine.

From the *Concise Oxford Dictionary*:

1. The scientific study of the human mind and its functions, esp. those affecting behavior in a given context.
2. A treatise on or theory of this.
3.a. the mental characteristics or attitude of a person or group
3.b. the mental factors governing a situation or activity (*the psychology of crime*)

Definition 1 has slyly added the idea of "affecting behavior". The original definition had nothing to do with this. The wish to control the minds and actions of others has entered into the equation.

From the *American Heritage Dictionary*:

1. The science that deals with mental processes and behavior.

2. The emotional and behavioral characteristics of an individual or group.

These definitions have further altered the true meaning. In actual practice, modern psychology deals almost exclusively with physiology (brain chemistry, neurology, genetics) and the behavior of the biological organism (stimulus-response), completely disregarding and ignoring the mind (man's inner self, and more to the point, man's true and vital self). The dictionaries will sooner or later remove the concept of "mind" completely from the definition following the lead of "official" psychology as taught in western universities and colleges.

Members of the educational establishment write the dictionaries, and the educational establishment is entrenched in modern psychological theories. Let's return to the correct definition of the word.

Adhering to the strict definition of the word, psychology would involve the study of man's invisible world as described above, and nothing else. By definition this is what the study would deal with. This is not an opinion or bias. This is according to exactly what the word means and nothing else. Of course, relations to behavior could be studied, and relations to brain activity could be studied, but the subject in itself, by definition is or should be the study of the mind or soul. A more correct name for the modern subjects of psychology and psychiatry would be "people control" because that's what they actually are. They are subjects involving how to alter thoughts, attitudes and behavior. The intention is to control people. That in a nutshell is the purpose of

behaviorism. Naturally governments and totalitarians love the subject. They also fund it in large way.

A Legitimate Study of the Mind

What would a study of the mind entail? It would investigate the nature, functioning, and potentials of man's inner and invisible mental activity. This would encompass such things as awareness, attention, intention, imagination and concentration. It would develop techniques for any individual to first, become aware of these functions, and to also strengthen and expand their use and control of these functions. It would also investigate the *actual source* of the problems anyone experiences with their own mind. Again, these things do exist, can be observed by anyone caring to examine *their own mind*, and involve a tremendous uncharted area of possible exploration, investigation, codification and summarizing.

Freudian psychology and psychotherapy, despite all its faults, at least recognized and partially examined this realm. For a subject calling itself the "science of the mind" to omit all this is a huge failure of modern psychology. It's actually absurd and would be laughable if the results of what they do weren't so insidious. It is equally laughable that many of these overly-educated boobs talk together as if they are the absolute pinnacle of truth about the subject of psychology. Sadly, too many others accept their claims and treat them as if they actually deserve respect, support and admiration. They don't.

This has nothing to do with mysticism, spiritualism (communicating with the dead), astral travel, OBE (out-of-body experiences), or psychic phenomena. It's not that these don't or can't exist, but a serious and scientific examination of the mind need not involve or explain these things.

It might eventually, but it isn't necessary. The point is you *do have a mind*. It is more *you* than anything else. You can take away your possessions, your family, your friends, your job, your arms, your legs, your torso, your ears, your nose, your jaw, your skull, and the one thing that remains, which always remains, and which is closest to your basic identity, is your *mind*. This is the invisible space and activity you are aware of every second of every day and that most people experience as existing "in their head". This realm has been grossly ignored by modern psychological studies and theories to our continual detriment and harm.

Some of this may be hard for some readers to understand or accept because an actual study and involvement with the mind isn't done at all under the current subject of psychology. It's strangely absent from most modern concepts of Man. This concept has been largely eradicated from the "modern world view".

Notions of the mind and related ideas about it have been falsely equated to "religion," "spiritualism," or "mysticism". We each have a mind. You know it, and I know it. We each experience it and its many various aspects as mentioned above. This is very simple and straightforward.

Modern psychology, due to absurd notions, flawed presumptions, intellectual dullness, observational weakness, blatant prejudice, and tremendous financial concerns ignores the mind completely, and *instead* concentrates on physiology, and analyzing and controlling animal behavior and responses to environmental factors. It's not that you don't have a body and use it to play your part in life. You do. There *is* physiology, and the environment *does* affect each and every one of us. But the current subject *pretends* to be a study of the mind and Man, and having failed completely at that has abandoned and finally denied the very existence of Man's mind. Worse, it pretends to be the *final word on the subject*, all the while attacking and suppressing any honest study or subject that deals with the actual field of the mind.

Evolutionists do not appear to see the difference between the matter part of an organism and the life part, which animates it. They seem to think that the organism itself is life. Psychology suffers a similar problem of understanding.

Modern psychology and psychiatry claim validity by posturing as "science". They claim to "study Man as an object of investigative science". They fail at this because any *legitimate* science should and would take into account *all* aspects of the subject it deals with. A valid science would not choose to omit a major body of data from its analysis, which is what they have done with the mind.

Dealing with, examining, and limiting observations to a specific *smaller* realm of data, while ignoring a very large area of other data, which it finds inconvenient because it fails to conform to their pet theories, is exactly what has been done by the modern fields of psychology and psychiatry. Failing to take the *entire* subject matter into

143

account has resulted in incorrect theories, faulty observations, flawed basic assumptions, and unworkable results.

Considering that every decent, creative, and wonderful thing in existence in the physical world started as an *idea* in the invisible and unobservable *mind* of someone should make this denial of the mind by "modern science" a major cause for alarm. This is doubly true when one also considers that every problem in society largely has its source in actual problems with an individual mind.

Education and the environment may heavily influence problems with crime, violence, abuse, and sexual deviancy, but ultimately the final basic source of these problem areas resides in the individual minds of people.

The Harmful Results of Denying the Mind

When the mind is denied, so ultimately is every good and decent thing that emanate from it including creativity, self-determinism, responsibility, morality, reason, and a value of life itself. The current decadent notion of man without a mind or inner personality, considered only as an animal or a biological organism has been institutionalized into the theories and practices of modern civilization in the media, sociology, education, government, economics, health, and of course, psychology and psychiatry.

This has had disastrous consequences in the form of increasing crime, divorce, violence, and decreasing levels of education, morality, personal responsibility, social stability and sanity. Simply, when the source of life itself for the individual and society is denied, oppressive practices parading as "science" surface and the quality of

144

life and sanity rapidly deteriorates. This is the exact condition of modern western civilization. Psychiatric lobotomy, electric shock treatment, psychoactive drugs, behavioral manipulation, mass population control, and social development instead of intellectual education in the schools serve as a few examples.

It has become popular in modern society for people to toss off, giggle about, ridicule and flippantly criticize any alternative subject of the mind (i.e. yoga, meditation, ritual magic, Rosicrucianism, Scientology, etc.) It is *in vogue* to consider these weird and unusual. And true enough, some of them *are* weird. But the only really weird and unusual thing is that modern man is so dull and heavily indoctrinated that he is almost completely incapable of a) looking at anything fairly, b) getting involved in it more than superficially, c) examining it in some detail, d) remaining honest about what he observes and e) deciding for himself based upon accurate personal observations. This reduction in mental and observational ability is also a result of modern educational practices. These practices are direct descendants of modern psychological theories that view man as a "social organism", and tend to ignore his intellectual and cognitive abilities and development (i.e. aspects of a mind).

A leading psychological text begins by very carefully saying that today the word "psychology" does not refer to the mind or soul, and "has to be studied by its own history", since it no longer refers to the soul, or even to the mind. The *Diagnostic and Statistical Manual (DSM-IV)*, the psychiatric bible of "mental disorders" states,

Although this volume is titled the Diagnostic and Statistical Manual of Mental Disorders, the term mental disorder unfortunately implies a distinction between "mental" disorders and "physical" disorders that is a reductionistic anachronism of mind/body dualism.

They readily admit ignoring the "mind" as a thing of itself to be studied or understood. The current subject is spiritually bankrupt and all that emanates from it denies life, and everything positive about humanity. The logical conclusion of modern psychological theory is that man is an animal to be genetically bred, controlled, herded, and placed into suitable environments. This is the approach of the modern social planner and behavioral controller. These are the guys who governments fund, support and listen to. Is it any wonder things aren't going so well on planet Earth?

Mr. P.D. Ouspensky says it well:

To begin with I must say that practically never in history has psychology stood at so low a level as at the present time. It has lost all touch with its origin and its meaning so that now it is even difficult to define the term "psychology": that is, to say what psychology is and what it studies. And this is so in spite of the fact that never in history has there been so many psychological theories and so many psychological writings. - The Psychology of Man's Possible Evolution, 1950

He also adds that psychology may be the "oldest science and unfortunately, in its most essential features *a forgotten science.*" A brief look at history is in order so the reader can understand more of what a true subject of psychology might entail.

146

The History of Psychology

For thousands of years psychology existed under the name of philosophy. The Hindu *Vedas* contain the oldest record of man's examination of mind and spirit. In India all forms of *Yoga*, which are essentially psychology, are described as one of the six systems of philosophy. *Sufi teachings*, which again are chiefly psychological, are regarded as partly religious and partly metaphysical. In more modern times some version of these systems, still largely following in this same vein, can be found the subjects of Rosicrucianism, New Thought, Science of Mind, visualization techniques, practical magick, and Scientology.

If you found yourself flinching or reacting negatively to the mention of any of these subjects, such as Yoga, Rosicrucianism, Scientology, or any of the many other alternative approaches to the mind and reality, realize this is not necessarily because there is anything actually strange or weird about these subjects. It is often largely because modern psychology, psychiatry and affiliated proponents of modern materialistic "science" have successfully applied black PR to them to such a large degree. In fact, they have covertly attacked these subjects for most of this century. An intelligent and objective look into any of these fields, although sometimes initially confusing largely due to the newness of the subject and difference in approach to reality will result in a widened understanding of yourself (and Man in general). Granted, you do need to and in fact you MUST weed out some of the nonsense often added to these subjects. Once you do take an honest look though it should become very obvious that modern western psychology has little to do with that incredible universe that exists a few inches behind your forehead. It must be mentioned that over time most of these subjects and fields (i.e. Scientology, Rosicrucianism, Transcendental Meditation, etc) have most definitely suffered from some combination of a) gross alterations introduced by self-appointed leaders following internal power struggles, b) manipulation of views and information by the more influential members, c) the sad tendency of some of the not-too-bright members to dictate changes not part of the original information, and d) the use of the subject and field to exert thought control and behavioral manipulation on its members. These faults are observably true and easily seen in the recent history of Scientology, though these faults exist in all to some degree. Lastly though, don't throw out the baby with the bathwater. While these all have serious flaws, don't use that as an excuse to dismiss everything about them outright without any serious examination. It takes careful and serious examination to separate the valuable from the invaluable - and there are often much of both to be found.

The mind *has* been examined, studied, drilled and "expanded", at times to the point of excruciating detail within many fields (i.e. Tibetan Buddhist Yogic practices). This is not to say that due to language barriers and the passage of time, that the information has not been lost to minor or major degrees or that these studies weren't without many errors, serious flaws, biases and differing opinions to start with. The point is **not** whether any of these are perfect studies (none are) or whether any of them have completed the task of researching the mind (none have), but that the *possibility for such a study most surely exists,* has been done before in various ways and to differing degrees, and that *modern psychology (and psychiatry) has **nothing** to do with this field.*

The Fraud of Modern Psychiatry

Psychiatrists will argue and say they use "mental" criteria routinely to diagnose mental illness. They do. But we need to take a closer look at what they do.

They never observe the mind with an intention to empower or strengthen its capabilities. This is covered in detail elsewhere.

Man and his societies cannot achieve happiness or success when the most basic and true aspect of Man has been denied and oppressed through institutionalized flawed belief systems parading as "science".

Modern psychological theories, in the form of psychiatry, genetics, behavioral science, social science, (and used by humanists and atheists to justify their positions):

1) are completely false omitting the key part of the subject (the mind),
2) pretend to be authoritative when they are factually not this at all, and
3) having been accepted and adopted by most major social and government institutions, directly allow the possibility and existence of the oppressive treatment of humanity. Man is viewed as nothing more than a fancy animal, and is treated as an animal.

Ken Kesey's book, and the movie starring Jack Nicholson, *One Flew Over The Cuckoo's Nest*, is not simply a social analogy portraying modern society's dislike and ultimate destruction of anyone who

149

consistently upsets the status quo. It *is* this, but it also is exactly what the story line indicates.

It is a graphic story clearly showing the lack of humanity, oppression, coercion, brute force and destructiveness of the modern "mental health" field. Without the firm denial of Man and his mind, they're largely the same thing in the end, none of these things could ever occur.

The movie contains many situations where the status quo attempts to control those who choose to walk outside the system and force them back into line. Modern psychiatry and psychology primarily serve that function of control seemingly required by society and civilization. It is not about help and betterment. It has never been about help or betterment. It *should* be about help and betterment.

The Errors of Modern Science and the Human Mind

Any person seriously concerned about Man, his mind, and society needs to be aware of exactly how "science" views and deals with these things. "Science" is fundamentally a method of investigation. The term "science" or "scientific" is erroneously attached to many fields of "study" that have very little to do with an honest application of the "scientific method". The majority of the "social sciences" is a misnomer. Due to the nature of Man, his mind, and of all resulting social manifestations (i.e. groups of individual human beings); a "scientific" analysis of Man is quite impossible and useless.

The "scientific method" has been most successful with the hard physical sciences, such as physics, chemistry, electronics and engineering (applied physical science). In each of these the scientists observe phenomena, develop theories, construct test, conduct tests, observe test results,

150

alter the theories as necessary, re-test, and continue this until they can achieve the same results consistently. The goal is complete, one-hundred percent repeatability and consistency. This enables exact predictability and complete control of results. Thus, bridges stay up, radios tune into stations day after day, rockets fire and move the payload up into space, and so on. Most of what we enjoy in modern life is the result of direct applications of science in the realm of physics, chemistry or electronics.

Calling something "science" or trying to apply the scientific method to situations where total consistency and predictability are not possible is ludicrous. This is the case with people and society, with the subjects of psychology, psychiatry, and sociology. Additionally, the goal of the application of the scientific method in the raw sciences is complete, total control of the environment and results. That is the nature of the application of the scientific method in the pure sciences (and engineering). The desired aim is *control*. The aim is total control.

This concept is unworkable for human beings. The notion of controlling the environment and human society to complete and total predictability can only degrade to totalitarianism.

There is no sane, decent or empowering method possible for "social engineering". The idea is actually absurd.

What *is* needed with people is empowering them with education, increasing mental ability, and expanding the powers of their individual intelligence.

You can put two people in the same exact environment and they will "react" or respond two different ways. The

151

idea of establishing exact environments (i.e. experimental test conditions) and obtaining one-hundred percent consistent results with human beings from one to the next is ridiculous. It is a completely dumb notion.

"Science" as traditionally applied to the physical universe is useless when applied to human beings and their societies in the same way, with the aim to total predictability and control. In fact, it's worse than useless; it's very harmful to Man and his societies. It's not only that it can't work, but results are produced that are *worse* than if they did nothing at all.

The goal of science as applied to the physical sciences is incompatible with human beings and his or her societies. "Science" *per se* cannot be successfully applied in any traditional way that empowers, helps or assists Man to rise to higher states and conditions of existence.

"Science" can and has been applied to the physical environment to improve conditions benefiting Man's physical survival, but that is not at all the same as applying "science" to Man, his mind, and his societies. Few recognize this distinction. It is a very important and vital distinction.

The mastery gained over the environment through the physical sciences has had numerous and amazing benefits for Mankind. The same thing cannot be said for the fields of psychology, psychiatry and sociology, which claim to be "scientific" and following in the "scientific tradition". It is impossible to apply the scientific method to people and societies and obtain positive results. Look around. A few examples should suffice to show the inherent flaws of the current approach.

Example #1:

There is a book entitled *The Three Faces of Eve*. It is about a woman who had multiple personalities to the point where each was separate, markedly different, and unaware of what the others would think, decide, and do. At some point in the past psychiatrists and psychologists noticed this phenomena. Upon further investigation it was discovered that people with this condition, known as "Dissociative Identity Disorder" and earlier as "Multiple Personality Disorder", usually had traumatic early life experiences that acted to precipitate the condition. These were usually violent and often involved severe sexual abuse.

How does "science" handle this? "Science" wants to "learn" what "causes" it, what the various factors are, and how the various factors relate to each other and the overall condition. They want to quantify everything like all good scientists want to do. How do they do this? They are not content to study past cases. Reading stories of such cases and listening to personal anecdotes do not satisfy them. The only "scientific" way to do it is by setting up carefully planned experiments involving severe sexual abuse, violence, and personality shattering experiences, observing the "results" of these experiments, and re-testing based upon the observations of their previous testing. Of course this is grossly immoral and decadent by any standard of human decency, but these folks who demand such experiments in the "name of science" have never been known to possess the qualities of decency, compassion or morality. The same logic, moral justification and "scientific methodology" of a Dr.

Mengele, Nazi medical experimenter, is alive today with these folks.

Science *has* been a success when applied to the physical realm of matter and energy. Combine two chemicals under a certain temperature and pressure and the resulting reaction is the same if conditions are kept consistent. Drop a rock with a certain mass in a vacuum and it accelerates and reaches the same terminal velocity every time. Science gains knowledge and control over matter and energy by establishing theories, conducting experiments, observing results, re-theorizing, conducting more experiments, until the results of the experiments can be duplicated consistently every time. This approach doesn't work with people and societies, although this hasn't stopped a tremendous number of deluded psychiatrists, psychologists and social scientists from trying. Even the term "social scientist" is downright absurd. It's an oxymoron. The two words cannot be put together in the same phrase and make any sense, at least not to a truly sensible person.

Continuing with our example of Eve, enter the CIA and other secretive government organizations. What purpose could a government intelligence agency have for a spy, agent or courier who could be numerous different personalities, all of which were quite unaware of what the others were thinking and doing and all of whom could be controlled by intelligence agency superiors? To the demented minds of these types of people the creation of such wonderful spies and agents would be a dream-come-true. So naturally they (probably) spent much time and money attempting to understand the mechanics of multiple personalities and creating their "perfect spy". Their excuse was "national security". The psychiatrists excuse was "gaining knowledge" and "understanding" the "true functioning of Man". Both of their excuses are nothing more than intellectual justifications for moral decadence, an utter lack of compassion and extreme harm to their fellow human beings.

They couldn't do this out in the open, because taking two to six year old children, submitting them to torture, sexual abuse, and extreme violence is not something the majority of humanity considers acceptable. Realize they wanted to "understand" completely the mechanics of the creation of multiple personality disorder, and develop the ability to successfully apply their theories and methods with *exact results*.

This is the "scientific method" applied to one phenomena of human life. They wanted to understand all the variables. They wanted to *intentionally* bring about multiple personalities, using all the means necessary, to obtain their "perfect spies". How did they do this? How are they probably now still doing this? They apply the methods of "science" to people, and experiment within the context of the subject (i.e. sexual abuse, torture, pain, degradation, etc.).

Realize they almost never experiment in the direction of helping, improving or empowering the individual, but instead almost always experiment to bring out the most horrific and degraded of possible human qualities. They do this for "pure science", "national security", "bringing about order" and other absurd abstract notions, which make total sense to them within the context of their deluded view of reality.

Obviously they must ensure there is absolutely no way they can be tied to what they are doing. They would need

155

covers. They would need groups who *already* involve themselves in such activities.

The following areas have probably been used as covers for such experiments:

CIA MK-Ultra mind control experiments conducted in Canada under the supervision of psychiatrist Dr. Ewen Cameron.

Black Magic Cults - Cult Ritual Abuse

Prostitution rings

Snuff films/ S & M / child pornography business

Child kidnapping & the human slave trade

The CIA would have had to make contacts and associations with very unsavory folks to carry out their plans. They did and probably still do. It would all be very "hush-hush", denied completely and they would probably do whatever they had to do to maintain their appearance of innocence and non-involvement. The utter fantastic nature of it all is their primary protection. Who would believe anyone, much less members of our own government, could or would do such things.

Black magic cults were probably infiltrated or *created*, so that severe violence, sexual abuse and emotional trauma to young children could be enacted, controlled, manipulated, and results carefully observed and recorded. Total "scientific control" would be required. Naturally these areas would also act as "recruiting pools" for their future spy resources. Cult ritual abuse *does* exist, but it exists today *much more* than it ever would have otherwise without the activities of these "intelligence" agencies and psychiatrists.

See what is actually occurring here. The psychiatrists first *create* the conditions, using the pretense of "gaining knowledge", and then come along and pretend to understand it and supply solutions to the problems they largely created in the first place, but which they deny all association with, and instead blame on "natural" and "self-existing" "mental illness" and "psychological disorders". If they had simply stayed out of it from the start the situations wouldn't exist to the degree that they do today. The same is true for violence, crime, immorality, and lone-nut assassins, who each always had undergone psychiatric treatment before committing their crime most likely in association with some covert intelligence agency psychological programmer. They will *never* "solve" these things. It is *their* theories and practices that largely *create* these things! If you believe otherwise you are as deluded as they are. If psychiatry and its influences could suddenly and magically be removed from every area of society, you would not believe the sudden change for the better in society and the improved individual "mental health" of people but back to the psychological "scientists".

To "understand" they would have had to test and *create* the conditions. They would have had to initiate very exact and controlled situations. The "scientists" would have wanted to ascertain just *how severe* an emotional shock was necessary to cause "dissociation", *how many* severe shocks were needed to create a permanent separation of a distinct "personality", how many *distinct personalities* could be created, and what type abuse was necessary to keep the personalities *operational*, separate and distinct. What type shock does the creation of dissociated personalities require?

157

Forced intercourse with pain and bleeding, physical abuse, torture, mutilation, sleep deprivation, food deprivation, sensory deprivation, murder of pets and even loved ones in plain sight of a young child, torture and murder of "friends" in plain sight, degrading activities such as smearing feces and urine all over their bodies, defecating on them, urinating on them, extreme verbal abuse and attacks, and on and on. Multiple personalities don't come about because a little boy loses his favorite comic book or a little girl loses her favorite doll. It takes *severe* trauma of a continuing and brutal nature. This requires abuse capable of reducing a human being to a complete animal devoid of all sense, reason, hope, love, care or any positive human qualities. It requires a complete destruction of the person's mind, emotions, and sense of self. They also discovered that for the dissociation to be most effective the initial major shocks must occur under the age of six. They probably discovered this by repetitive, continual, and intense abuse of many innocent children. "When you've got to know, you've got to know . . ." Who am I to stop the forward progress of science? (extreme sarcasm here)

But according to the CIA "intelligence" mentality, "we must protect our national security", and to the experimenting psychiatrists, "we must apply 100% objective science toward understanding the true nature of Man". Be sure of one thing, they submitted innocent children to horrendous treatments in their search and continuing actions to "understand the mechanics of MPD" and to maintain their "perfect" spies. They all deserve to be drawn and quartered in plain public view and I honestly pray there will be a very special place in eternal Hell for all of them! No

158

penalty would be too severe for what they have done, regardless of their "sensible" excuses and justifications of "science" and "national security". As far as I am concerned, any group that would condone such activities doesn't deserve to be protected or maintained.

The thing these type folks *never* seem to be capable of understanding is that Man can be so many different things. If Man is treated like a mindless animal he will tend to act like one. But if Man is treated like a thinking, capable, and responsible being, and given the tools to become such a being, he also tends to act this way. It isn't a matter of figuring out what man *actually is*, as the modern proponents of "science" claim to be doing, but more deciding what we *want him to be*. Because Man *can be anything*, from the very absolute worst to the most fantastic best! Modern psychiatry and psychology view Man as an animal, as a biological organism, as a beast to be controlled, and *not as a mind*. Viewing Man as an animal will send him further *down* in that direction. Viewing Man *as a mind*, with all that entails, will send him *up* to greater heights and possibilities and in another direction entirely.

These "scientists" want to "know" and will do just about anything to "increase their knowledge". Apparently, various intelligence organizations have worked with and through various illegal activities and organizations to conduct their experiments and continue their covert spy operations, all the while working with "brilliant" psychiatrists and social "scientists". These psychiatric "professionals" hold degrees and professorships at the best colleges and universities. They are members and leaders of influential psychiatric associations and

159

publications. But more to the point, these people are and always have been the worse type of criminals. They have absolutely no sense of humanity or decency, despite everything they pretend and assert. They are despicable examples of humanity pretending to be something else entirely. They are most certainly not decent, honest human beings, and they will deserve completely whatever ill fate finally befalls them.

The goal of the psychiatrists, psychologists and intelligence organizations is to CONTROL human behavior. They want to be able to control human behavior just as the physical scientist controls chemicals, electronics, or metals. They want 100% consistent results all of the time. They want people to behave as they feel they should. The thing they always lose sight of is that human beings are *not* simply chemicals, electrons or energy. You can't simply push on a human being a certain way and have him keep going in the same direction, like a rock or brick on a frictionless surface. People are not simply matter and energy. Human beings are entities of *consciousness* with thought, awareness, will, attention, purposes, goals, imagination, responsibility and creativity. Human beings don't simply do what they are told. They decide and *then* act. They learn through education, personal desire and intention. Trying to force human beings into a mold conforming to the same paradigm as that which understands the physical sciences is severely flawed and has disastrous consequences for people and society. People *aren't* rocks. People *aren't* electrons running through a wire in an electric circuit. Treating them as such goes nowhere. Actually that's not quite true; it's worse; treating them as such causes individual deterioration, personal disasters and widespread social failure.

The methods and goals of science as applied to the raw physical universe of matter and energy are incompatible and unworkable in the realm of Man, his mind, and his societies. One-hundred percent total control and predictability of atoms, chemicals, and electrons is useful and works. One-hundred percent total control and predictability of people and societies is not useful and doesn't work. In fact it's a degrading and idiotic idea. But that is the trend of modern psychology, psychiatry, and sociology. These fields are filled with many powerful people, with large salaries, and with lots of letters after their names (i.e. Ph.D.) who are basically fools. In too many cases they are nasty fools.

Example #2:

Another example is religion. Social psychologists, sociologists, and government types noticed at some point that certain people have committed really strange and despicable crimes due to their religious or intense personal beliefs. This is very true. People have done many strange things in the name of some religion. There was obviously some relationship between the religious structure, beliefs and resultant actions. But again, simply studying past cases and depending on anecdotal evidence wouldn't be enough for them.

Sociologists, psychologists and psychiatrists wanted to "understand" and "learn" how religion can be used to *control* people. "How can we use religion and beliefs to get people to do what we want?" "How far will they go in the name of a religion?" What are the variables involved?

How do these variables interact and relate? There was never any intention to ascertain whether there is any validity to the subjects of various religions.

There is much evidence that the Jonestown mass murder, called mass suicide in the media, involving Jim Jones and the People's Temple was a CIA experiment in group mind control gone badly. Mass quantities of various psychiatric drugs were discovered at Jonestown after the event. Psychiatrists *were* involved.

Apparently "scientists" wanted to ascertain what people could be made to believe, and more importantly, what they could be manipulated into *doing* in the "name of" some religious creed or idea. The wanted to "study" by direct experimentation under controlled conditions, using the scientific method, the relationship of belief, conviction, and worship to actions, to the point of committing murder and suicide. Who knows where else and in what other situations they have done similar things? Be sure though, they have done it. That is the nature of "science" when applied to people and societies. Test-test-test and forget about one's conscience, decency and morality.

Again, to "learn" they had to "experiment". Realize this experimentation along these lines can only be highly oppressive and degrading to the victims. It serves no honest or decent useful purpose. It is another example of a crime against humanity, but hidden again behind deluded notions of "science", "the country's best interests" and "gaining knowledge". The real sick thing is that it makes perfect sense to those perpetrating these horrendous abuses. They don't think they are doing

162

anything wrong, and ironically, some of them feel they are the most "dedicated", "honest" and "patriotic" folks compared to the rest of us. They "sacrifice a few to benefit the many, because it's the nature of war . . ." They are severely deluded, and cause incredible harm to people and society.

Human history is primarily a comedy of errors. It is only one series of possibilities, stretched out over time and space, out of an infinite possible variety of alternatives. These "scientists" examine one small aspect of Man's history or culture, take it to be "the way things are", call the subject anthropology, and experiment along a similar path in an attempt to "understand" and "control". They never quite understand that what Man has been in the past too often has been largely due to oppression, ignorance (lack of education), deception (mis-education) and the abusive control of past kings, dictators, and Churches. Man has *never* been allowed to exist in an empowering environment that acknowledges and encourages all the good about him. That is equally true today. For "social science" to study and investigate these past instances of social circumstances with the idea of actually learning anything useful about human beings is absurd. It's dull people conducting equally dull studies. These people are largely morons despite all their complex studies and assertions.

They make another major error in theory and practice. The modern views of "social science" too often include the notion that "societies" and "groups" are actual organisms or entities with a life and existence of their own. Some asinine theorists (i.e. Hegel, Karl Marx, and John Dewey) even assert that the "social entity" is MORE important and has more validity than the individuals!

163

Therefore they try to envision and create various social structures to bring about new, "better", and alternate conditions. They talk about the "ills of society", "social decay", "the State", "social tension", and "social harmony" as if these were real things. There is *no* "social" organism. There is *no* "organic whole of all life". These are concepts, abstractions, and ideas that exist ONLY in someone's head. They have no real basis in observable fact outside of the ideas certain men hold about them. And placing these concepts in positions of importance senior to the life of individual human beings is ludicrous and always results in harm to various members of the civilization involved.

The only *actual thing* is a human being, a unique individual mind, a person. All else is pretty much conceptions and ideas in his and others' minds. Any society, group or civilization is ONLY the sum total of all the individual people comprising it. What makes any society, group or civilization what it is involves only the *sum total* of all the notions, ideas, beliefs, values, decisions, responsibility, self-determinism, goals, and actions of the individual people involved. If anyone seriously wants to make a better society, civilization or world, the *only* correct and successful approach is to *first make better people*. There is no other way to do it. Strangely, no one even considers this approach today. Possibly the idea is too "simple" for the overly complex intellectuals of today. They would rather spend endless energy and time fabricating complex laws, legislation and social mandates, in their perverted attempts to "coerce" or "enable" Man to "evolve" and behave "appropriately". These modern politicians, social theorists and group psychologists are dolts. They spend all their time trying to come up with the "ideal social system", while continually ignoring the only thing that will ever bring about any real lasting improvement, the betterment and empowerment of the minds of individual men and women. And that they don't deal with at all.

Example #3:

Another example is electric shock treatments.

The story of electric shock began in 1938, when Italian psychiatrist Ugo Cerletti visited a Rome slaughterhouse to see what could be learned from the method that was employed to butcher hogs. In Cerletti's own words,

"As soon as the hogs were clamped by the [electric] tongs, they fell unconscious, stiffened, and then after a few seconds they were shaken by convulsions. During this period of unconsciousness (epileptic coma), the butcher stabbed and bled the animals without difficulty....

"At this point I felt we could venture to experiment on man, and I instructed my assistants to be on the alert for the selection of a suitable subject."

Cerletti's first victim was provided by the local police - a man described by Cerletti as "lucid and well-oriented." After surviving the first blast without losing consciousness, the victim overheard Cerletti discussing a second application with a higher voltage. He begged Cerletti, "Non una seconda! Mortifiere!" ("Not another one; it will kill me!").

Ignoring the objections of his assistants, Cerletti increased the voltage and duration and fired again. With the "successful" electrically induced convulsion of his victim, Ugo Cerletti brought about the application of hog-slaughtering skills to humans, creating one of the most brutal techniques of psychiatry.

At no point had anyone ever observed a human being benefiting, improving, becoming happier, or expanding in responsibility from an electric shock. What depraved stream of logic determines that submitting a human being to a hog-slaughtering technique is "therapeutic" or "helpful"?

But this is natural and business as usual for psychiatrists.

This is another example of "scientists" experimenting on human beings in an attempt to "learn" something, and to control. There has never been any basis in "science" for electric shock treatments. Yes, sure it changes people, but smashing them in the head with a baseball bat would also change them. Sticking bamboo shoots under their fingernails would surely change them.

Psychiatrists and scientists have come up with many theories to "explain" how ECT "helps cure mental illness", but these are nothing more than fairy tales. And while reading a Grimm fairy tale hurts nobody, the modern fairy tales of the psychiatrists and psychologists are not so innocuous. Electric shock and other psychiatric methods cause severe harm while parading as "modern science", "cures" and "therapy".

Human beings respond and react to force, whether that force be physical, chemical or electrical. *Never* is the application of any force helpful or empowering to the individual. Modern "science" is rooted in applying force or energy of some sort to some situation to bring about a change or new condition. This is fine and desirable in the pure physical sciences. Modern medicine, electronics, and various fields of engineering have made great strides in improving the physical condition of mankind. But force doesn't produce any decent or desirable results when applied to human beings. The result is *always* confusion, degradation, loss of personal responsibility, and chaos.

What works with people is appealing to understanding, communication, and interacting with the functions of the mind of the person. The approach of the modern psychiatrist, psychologist and social scientist is to apply the same notions of the physical sciences to the realm of Man, his mind and society. It doesn't "work". It will *never* "work". The only result will always be harm, failure, deterioration and the collapse of individuals and society. Take a look around. What Man lacks more than anything is an *understanding and science of his own mind*.

The successful "science" of physical matter and energy involves applying differing types of forces to bring about new conditions in controlled situations. It works in the realm of physical matter and energy. It does not work in the realm of human beings, human minds, and societies. The application of force to individual minds and societies has no possible positive rendition. Freedom, responsibility, self-determinism, morality and decency are incompatible with force, and therefore with any attempt at a scientific "solution" to Man and his societies. It simply can't and won't ever get anywhere decent or desirable for the people as a whole. Communism was an attempt at a "scientific" study and application to human beings and society. It depended almost completely on force, and obviously failed miserably, as it only could.

167

Force, and therefore "science", is unworkable with people.

For "science" to work with human beings and societies, it must drastically alter its approach. There is nothing wrong with "science". In fact it is wonderful if used correctly. There is everything wrong with the manner in which purported "science" currently views and attempts to deal with human beings. The "scientific method" *is* extremely useful, but that isn't what is used in the subjects of psychology, psychiatry and the "social sciences". These fields have attached themselves to the concept of "science" in an attempt to gain legitimacy while actually promoting bias, opinion, and false notions about Man and his mind under a facade of "research" and "objective science".

First, Man's mind is NOT matter or energy, The brain that houses the mind is matter and the chemical reactions in the brain are energy but the mind is best described as spirit and the energy thereof is from God to man. It doesn't function as if it is made of matter or energy, and cannot be "solved" by treating it as such. All attempts to do so will result in ultra-controlled, totalitarian systems with the individual oppressed.

Second, the "mind" of Man and all it is must be recognized as the *primary* aspect of value and importance with Man and his societies.

"Science" has never examined, with an aim to "solve" and "improve", *the mind of Man.*

- What is it?
- How does it work?
- What are its functions?

168

- What are its problems?
- How can it be bettered?

It *has* been investigated, when considered at all, primarily from a viewpoint of how to *control* it. But modern psychiatry and psychology have largely abandoned all notions of a mind and instead concentrate on biochemistry, behavior, environmental factors (i.e. stimulus-response), and genetics. This will lead nowhere.

Man is primarily a *mind*. A mind is aware, experiences, thinks, chooses, determines, imagines, conceives, considers, believes, conceptualizes, places attention, intends, sets goals, exerts discipline, adheres to accepted codes of conduct (morality) and can act responsibly according to self-determined decisions and agreements. THESE things need to be seriously acknowledged, investigated, studied, tested, and understood with an aim towards *empowering the individual*. The scientific method *could* be applied to these aspects of the human mind but never has been. There is no extant subject dealing with these things anywhere within the traditional confines of modern education and thought. The aim of *control* would be one of "self-control", the control of one's *own* mind in all its aspects.

One problem here is that for all practical purposes the mind and all its functions and contents are invisible. A thought can't be measured. An emotion can't be placed in a test tube. Imagination can't be weighed. A goal can't be quantified. A human intention can't be objectively viewed and examined with statistical analysis. Feelings of love, hate, anger or enthusiasm cannot be detected outside of the behaviors associated with them.

169

It's also difficult to know whether people undergoing "mental" experiments are doing what they say they are doing with their minds. This has been a real major stumbling block for the modern "scientist" familiar only with dealing with visible, tangible and physical things. The "things" of the mind are *not* visible or detectable in the same way as any other object of observation in the entire physical universe. Simply, the mind is of an entirely different nature and adheres to different laws. Anyone honestly observing their own mind will come to this same conclusion, and nobody else can ever do this for you. You are the only one who experiences your mind *as your mind* in the way you experience it. You know your thoughts, feelings, ideas, hopes, and goals are real, yet these are completely invisible to everyone else, and *vice versa.* "Objective" science is impossible when dealing with a mind because it can't be observed *as it is* by anyone except the person whose mind it is. This doesn't make scientific examination impossible, but it does necessitate a different approach to addressing the subject. The scientific approach used in the physical sciences can't be easily transferred to the realm of the mind where everything about it is invisible to objective detection.

Early psychologists from Germany in the late 1800s, Wilhelm Wundt and his followers, decided, "since the human mind and inner states cannot be observed or measured directly, we will ignore them, not deal with them at all and only concern ourselves with behavior". And so it has been ever since. It's not that the mind doesn't exist; each of us knows it does from our own direct personal experience, but the entire approach of "modern science" with this subject has *ignored and denied the mind* as a factor of importance and object of study. Considering that every decent, great or noble thing originated as an idea in the mind of some man or woman should make it fairly obvious that discarding the mind of Man as part of the basic underlying philosophical bent of various modern "social sciences" cannot ever have positive results.

There needs to be an honest scientific examination of the mind of Man with an aim towards understanding, solving and improving it in all its aspects. But it must be dealt with on its *own level*, within its *own context*, and addressing its *own functions*. Trying to understand it and what it does from a framework of physical matter and energy is useless. As an example take the conservation of energy theory. This states that no matter or energy can be created newly, but only its form can be altered. This is not true at all in the realm of mind. Man's imagination is constantly creating newly out of nothing....symphonies, plays, books, inventions, and so on. The functions of Man's mind are radically different than anything else observable "out there" in the material universe.

- What is attention?
- How can it be strengthened, concentrated, directed, intensified, or reduced at will?
- What drills are necessary to assist a person to become aware of and control their own attention?
- What is the nature of concentration?
- Can it be improved?
- How so?
- What exercises or drills lead to bettered concentration?

171

- What is imagination?
- What different types of imagination are there?
- Can it be improved?
- How?
- What are goals?
- How do they relate to reality, intention and determination?
- Can intention and determination be increased?
- How much?
- How so?

This list of questions can easily get quite long. The mind is a completely unexamined and uncharted area requiring extensive investigation. The only way to effectively improve qualities of a mind is with "mental" techniques. Such techniques are strangely missing in the current fields related to the mind.

Many supposed "mental illnesses" such as depression, anxiety and compulsions are nothing more than a severe inability of the person to control and direct their own attention. This is not said to minimize the seriousness of the condition to the person who "suffers" from these things or to suggest they aren't real. They are real, but they don't exist as "illnesses" or "diseases". They *are* conditions, but are not adequately addressed and handled by a medical or biological approach. They are definitely NOT "physical illnesses". If a person truly learned how and was able to control where they allowed their own attention to fall, whether on external things and situations, or upon internal ideas, feelings or sensations, the power of these supposed "mental illnesses" would greatly decrease.

The only real "mental illness" in the world today is modern Man's almost complete lack of any understanding about his own mind, how to deal with it, and how to learn to gain control over it and everything it is capable of doing for and to him. Ultimately it *is* a matter of *control*, but of *self-control*, over that immense universe of thought we each possess, seemingly, though not necessarily, a few inches behind our foreheads.

The modern approaches of psychiatry and psychology don't assume self-control is possible because they don't even consider your mind exists. To many of them the mind is nothing but an accidental by-product of chemical reactions in a brain, and an annoying by-product at that. It seems they would be happiest if it didn't exist at all, and many of them are trying to bring such a view about.

The mind *exists*. It *is* invisible. It does things that no matter or energy anywhere in the entire universe does. It's aware, it conceptualizes, it sets goals, it establishes values, it chooses, it intends, it appreciates, it admires, and it initiates action (to mention only a few). No example of matter or energy located anywhere in space or time, which is the subject of the physical sciences, does what a mind does. Someday some of these brilliant "scientists" may finally notice this and change their approach to the subject.

A mind and all it does is *not* similar in nature to any of the objects of physical reality that a mind perceives and is aware of. So why treat it as if it is similar? This is simply a huge error of viewpoint on the subject. It is a basic assumption taken by the majority of people, which is just plain incorrect.

Also, the purpose of such a scientific investigation cannot be to manipulate, control, force or dictate belief, thought, ideas or actions against the will of the person. People need to be educated into the discoveries of a scientific examination of the mind, and each individual placed in *control of their own mind* with tools to understand and improve their own mind. Too often others decide what the beliefs, attitudes and behaviors should be. This must stop or this civilization will continue to decline and fail.

The current "scientific" approach to Man and his mind is wrong, 180 degrees wrong in the opposite direction of what could and would help individual people and also thereby, their societies, which are nothing more than groups of *individual people*. There will never be success viewing and treating Man as only so much matter, energy, chemicals, atoms and electrical reactions.

This is why psychiatry can only fail. It views and treats Man as matter and energy, and their only "solution" is force, because force is the only "solution" in the realm of matter and energy. You can't get a rock to move by appealing to its "understanding". It moves only by brute force. You *can* get a person to move by appealing to "understanding". "Understanding" is one of these "mind qualities". People *aren't* rocks, *shouldn't* be treated as such, but this is functionally the view and approach taken by psychiatry, which *does* depend completely upon *force*; physical force by involuntary commitment, restraints, deprogramming techniques, lobotomy, and strait jackets, electrical force by electric shock treatments, chemical force by powerful, brain-altering and mind-altering psychotropic drugs.

174

At no point does the "modern scientific" approach consider, acknowledge, address or better *any human mind* on the level of and within the context of the functions of a human mind. In fact, modern psychiatry flat-out *denies* the existence of a "mind". This basic philosophical error of psychiatry in understanding and "treating" Man, *the denial of the human mind*, makes any attempts to improve Man doomed to fail within the context of their grossly flawed theories and methods.

Of course, psychiatry's goal has never been to "help", empower or bring about increased happiness, success, self-determinism or responsibility in any individual human being. Their goal has always only been about controlling behavior, behavior that others find objectionable or inconvenient. This explains why governments and intelligence agencies have worked with and funded psychiatry and modern psychology for so many years. Their goal is often also control of the thoughts, beliefs and actions of the people. Sadly, this is as true for American "democracy" as it is for any totalitarian regime such as communist China or a South American dictatorship. The common denominator of them all is control, and psychiatry and modern psychology supply them with important "tools" to achieve their aims. If the theories and methods of modern psychology and psychiatry led to individual personal expansion, happiness, mental stability, certainty, knowledge, freedom, responsibility, awareness and self-determined moral action, then no totalitarian government would ever have supported them. But then psychiatry and modern psychology *don't* lead to these things and governments *do* very much support them.

I Have a Special Gift for My Readers

I appreciate my readers for without them I am just another author attempting to make a difference. If my book has made a favorable impression please leave me an honest review. Thank you in advance for you participation.

My readers and I have in common a passion for the written word as well as the desire to learn and grow from books.

My special offer to you is a massive ebook library that I have compiled over the years. It contains hundreds of fiction and non-fiction ebooks in Adobe Acrobat PDF format as well as the Greek classics and old literary classics too.

In fact, this library is so massive to completely download the entire library will require over 5 GBs open on your desktop.

Use the link below and scan all of the ebooks in the library. You can select the ebooks you want individually or download the entire library.

The link below does not expire after a given time period so you are free to return for more books rather than clog your desktop. And feel free to give the link to your friends who enjoy reading too.

I thank you for reading my book and hope if you are pleased that you will leave me an honest review so that I can improve my work and or write books that appeal to your interests.

Okay, here is the link...

http://tinyurl.com/special-readers-promo

PS: If you wish to reach me personally for any reason you may simply write to mailto:support@epubwealth.com.

I answer all of my emails so rest assured I will respond.

Meet the Author

Dr. Harry Jay is Director of Research for AppliedMindSciences.com, a mental health and mind research group of Applied Web Info, and is the author of over 100 books and research papers as a behavioral scientist.

In his 32-year career, Dr. Harry Jay has contributed many new mental health treatment treatments and protocols using some of the new advances he has discovered in Energy Psychology.

He specializes in addictions of all kinds, sexual abuse, child predation and gender relationships.

He is also a board member to ePubWealth.com and serves on the science committee assisting non-fiction science writers in book publishing and promotion.

As a leading behavioral scientist, he provides profiling services to the company's ForensicsNation.com unit as well as criminal psychology research to aid in identifying and apprehending child predators and cyber-criminals of all kinds.

He resides in Southern Utah and enjoys the outdoors, fishing and photography.

Visit some of his websites

http://www.AddMeInNow.com
http://www.AppliedMindSciences.com
http://www.AppliedWebInfo.com
http://www.BookbuilderPLUS.com
http://www.BookJumping.com
http://www.EmailNations.com
http://www.EmbarrassingProblemsFix.com
http://www.ePubWealth.com
http://www.ForensicsNation.com
http://www.ForensicsNationStore.com
http://www.FreebiesNation.com
http://www.HealthFitnessWellnessNation.com
http://www.Neternatives.com
http://www.PrivacyNations.com
http://www.RetireWithoutMoney.org
http://www.SurvivalNations.com
http://www.TheBentonKitchen.com
http://www.Theolegions.org
http://www.VideoBookbuilder.com

Some Other Books You May Enjoy From ePubWealth.com, LLC Library Catalog

EPW Library Catalog Online
http://www.epubwealth.com/wp-content/uploads/2013/07/Leland-benton-private-turbo.pdf

EPW Library Catalog Download
http://www.filefactory.com/f/562ef3ea1a054f0a